Growing Up ASIAN

Teens Write About Asian-American Identity

By Youth Communication

Edited by Maria Luisa Tucker

Growing Up ASIAN

EXECUTIVE EDITORS
Keith Hefner and Laura Longhine

CONTRIBUTING EDITORS
Hope Vanderberg, Tamar Rothenberg, Clarence Haynes, Philip Kay, Vivian Louie, Rachel Blustain, Duffie Cohen, and Alexandra Ringe

LAYOUT & DESIGN
Efrain Reyes, Jr. and Jeff Faerber

COVER ART
YC Art Dept.

For reprint information, please contact Youth Communication.

ISBN 978-1-935552-35-2

Second, Expanded Edition

Printed in the United States of America

Youth Communication ®
New York, New York
www.youthcomm.org

Catalog Item #YD08-1

Table of Contents

Where Nobody Knows My Name

Sung Park 40

As the only Koreans in a white, upper class neighborhood, Sung and her family get the cold shoulder.

Beyond the Great Wall of Chinatown

Xiao Ling Zhong 44

Xiao Ling feels at home in Chinatown, but worries that living there prevents her from fully integrating into American life.

'Chinklish'

Winnie Tang 49

Winnie and her friends speak a mixture of Cantonese and English.

Wake-Up Call in Another World

Maria Zaman 53

When she visits her native Pakistan, Maria is appalled by the poverty she sees and decides to become involved in fighting it.

Unwelcome in the Hood

George Yi 59

In his new neighborhood, George is frequently taunted by black kids. But then a black youth befriends him, and belies the stereotype.

The Stranger in My House

May Mai 87

In the U.S., May's father changes from the fun and loving person she knew in China to a tired, distant, and angry man.

Chinese in America, American in China

Kim Hoang 93

When Kim visits her sister in Beijing, she is fascinated by the culture but also realizes how foreign it is to her.

Other Ways to Be Rich

Leneli Liggayu 98

By American standards, Leneli's relatives in the Philippines are poor; but they're rich in love and community.

Money Can't Buy Love

Lily Mai 105

Lily feels neglected by her hardworking immigrant parents, until she travels to China and sees the poverty they escaped.

A Short Cut to Independence

Anita Chikkaur 110

Anita is raised to believe that being a "good Indian girl" means having long hair. Then she gets a haircut.

Using the Book

Introduction

"Studying European and American history at school, I began to realize that I wasn't white like other kids," writes Victoria Law. "I didn't share a common past with them. But I didn't fit in with other Chinese people either." Victoria feels neither fully American nor fully Asian. She is stuck in the sometimes-lonely place in between, where all the writers in this book reside.

For the teen writers in this collection, just the term "Asian-American" suggests cultural conflict. It conjures up two different worlds separated by an ocean, two opposing sets of customs. They are pulled between their family's traditional culture and the freedoms of American teenagerhood. But these aren't stuffy essays about vague concepts of culture and identity. They are real-world stories of what those conflicts look like in the every-day lives of Asian-American teens; stories about immigration and disrupted families, strict parents, dating, language barriers, and prejudice.

In the opening story, Jordan Yue is frustrated by the "model minority" stereotype projected onto him by his parents and teachers. "They all had their pre-formed ideas about who I was supposed to be: a good, hardworking, quiet Asian kid," he writes. The stereotype, "labeled me as something I wasn't." Meanwhile, Luce Tang, the only Asian kid in her neighborhood, is shocked and angered when she gets called a "ch-nk" and "dog-eater" by strangers. Their stories, and others, prove that racism is more than a black-and-white thing.

Growing up Asian in America can be a battle at home, too. In "Daddy's Nicest Daughter," the author's mother tells her, "We are Indians, remember that, and Indians don't have boyfriends or girlfriends." But she still dreams of romance and begins dating behind her parents' back. A secret boyfriend, a screaming fight, and silent worry about arranged marriage ensue. Others teens describe how they reluctantly follow their parents' strict rules about dating—and everything else. "As much as I would like to dye my hair, stay out late, not worry about school, and have boyfriends the way my American friends do, I understand that there are valid reasons to follow many aspects of the Chinese culture," writes Ngan-Fong Huang.

A book about Asian-Americans wouldn't be complete without the story of immigration. First-generation immigrants write about nostalgia for their Eastern homelands—villages that hold the mystical appeal of a long-lost childhood. American-born writers are shocked by the poverty they see when they visit relatives in Asia for the first time. And several of our writers explain the toll that starting over in a new country has taken on their families. For example, May Mai writes that her father emigrated to the U.S. when she was little and then brought the rest of the family over six years later. May is initially happy that the family is reunited, but finds that her work-obsessed father, "had changed from the fun and loving person I'd known in China to a tired, strict, distant, and angry man."

The immigration experience also presents language barriers. Amy Huang tells the touching story of feeling lost in her English-language 4th grade classroom, and powerless against girls who tease her. "I hated myself for not being able to speak English—I couldn't do anything about my bullies since I couldn't communicate with the teacher." But she learns English much faster than her parents and eventually becomes the family's translator. Meanwhile, Winnie Tang and her friends employ their native tongue to their advantage. "My friends and I use Cantonese, a Chinese language, to communicate things that we don't want other people to know," she writes.

Writing about their families, their first loves, and their friends, the teens here show a diversity of Asian-American experience. They are new immigrants, American-born Chinese; Pakistani, Indian, and Korean. But whatever their roots, they are writing about something that many teens—Asian or otherwise—can relate to: trying to figure out who they are and where they fit in our multi-cultural world.

Names have been changed in the following stories: *Tongue-Tied, Thinking Twice About Race,* and *Ignoring the Stares.*

Fighting the 'Model Minority' Stereotype

By Jordan Yue

"You're good at math, right?"

Both Asian and non-Asian classmates have said that to me, throwing it out in casual conversation as we're walking to class. Actually, I'm just OK at math. But it bothers me that they seem to think I'd be a math whiz just because I'm Chinese-American and there's a common idea that Chinese—and Asians in general—are good at math. I feel like people have certain assumptions about me simply because when they look at me, they see "Chinese" or "Asian."

The stereotype goes beyond math skills. Asians are called the "model minority" because we're the minority group that people say succeeds best in America; according to the stereotype, we work hard, stay quiet, and don't cause trouble. An Asian student is valedictorian? No big surprise. According to the stereotype, we're both disciplined and naturally smart.

It's not like the stereotype comes from nowhere. In Chinese culture, for example, education and discipline are very important. Throughout Chinese history, scholars were the most respected people in society. Martial arts, tai chi, and Confucian principles also teach discipline, so it makes sense that discipline plays an important part in the culture. That might sound good to you, but the flip side is that we're also considered sexless (or at least the guys are), socially inept, and easily picked on. And even the "good" parts of the stereotype bug me, because I feel like people look at me and automatically see someone I'm not.

It was like people assumed I would get good grades and be obedient just because I was Asian.

Now, I'm not gonna front. In some ways I do fit this stereotype, at least the academic part. I go to Bronx Science High School in New York, a competitive school that you have to take a test to get into; more than 40% of my school is Asian. But in other ways, I feel like the stereotype isn't me, and even if I wanted to be that way and tried, I couldn't do it. I'm also mad at the reality behind the stereotype; at home, I get the kind of pressure to do well that really is common in Asian families. I feel like both outsiders and my own parents expect me to be the "model minority."

Ever since I can remember, I haven't matched people's expectations. I'm a third generation Asian-American—this means it was my great-grandparents who immigrated here—and in lots of ways I feel more American than Chinese. I don't speak Chinese. I like basketball. I listen mostly to hip-hop, reggae, blues, rock, and r&b. I hate going to school. I curse like a sailor. I'm interested in the latest sneakers coming out. I'm your typical New Yorker.

Back when I was a young'un, I wasn't treated warmly by most of the Asian kids in my neighborhood. They were mostly first and second generation Koreans and some Chinese; most of the kids' parents were immigrants, and some of the kids were, too. I didn't understand Chinese and I didn't speak with an accent, so they often accused me of trying to "be white." At school or playing ball in the neighborhood, they made it clear that I didn't fit in with them. Instead of hanging out with just Asian kids, I had friends who varied in race and I was a lunchroom table-hopper, trying out different groups.

At home, my parents expected me to be a good student. An 80 on a test wasn't good enough. It sometimes seemed that they wanted me to exceed some unspoken limit. For the most part, this didn't bother me. I did my work in school and didn't cause too many problems. Up through 7th grade I was relatively obedient and performed well throughout the year.

Still, my heroes were loner rebel characters like Han Solo, a leader of the Rebel Alliance in the Star Wars trilogy, and Wolverine of the X-Men. Wolverine is hotheaded, doesn't always listen to Cyclops or Professor X, and always seems pissed off and ready to fight because he was either misunderstood or treated wrongly. I looked up to these rebels, who were much more fascinating than the do-gooder, wholesome characters like Superman.

It wasn't until 8th grade that I started acting up in class. I wasn't doing as well in school, and my teachers started sending notes home to my parents. They got mad and yelled at me, so I'd yell back. I felt that my parents were simply putting more pressure on me rather than hearing me out. Not that I knew what exactly was bothering me; I just felt 8th grade was a waste of time. I was disruptive and made inappropriate comments in my classes and to teachers. At the time, I thought I was funny, even if classmates were telling me to shut up.

Although part of me was having fun, part of me was also angry. I felt that I couldn't fulfill my parent's expectations, or anyone else's. They all had their pre-formed ideas about who I was supposed to be: a good, hardworking, quiet Asian kid. I felt that nobody understood me and worse, no one cared to try.

I was angry at my parents, who I felt were blaming me without acknowledging their own contributions to my behavior. Sometimes they would hold up my friends as examples, telling me, "You should be doing as well as he does." All my Asian friends' parents did that, so I didn't feel singled out, but I didn't like my parents comparing me to my friends because we're different people.

The worse I felt, the angrier I got, and the more trouble I got in. I was acting out and not handing in my work, and my parents were furious over the letters they were getting about me cutting class. I wasn't happy with myself, but my parents yelling at me so much didn't exactly motivate me to make the right choices. I felt that I didn't fit in at home or at school, but I didn't know why or how to change the situation.

Then, the summer after 8th grade, I picked up a book called *Eastern Standard Time,* which is about Asian culture in America. The book brought to my attention the "model minority" stereotype and opened up a world of thought for me. The book said that the image of a studious, disciplined achiever was something that grew out of Asian values and suggested that it's both positive and negative.

I didn't have to choose between the total rebel or the total goody two-shoes. I could be a balance of both.

At first I thought I liked the idea of the model minority stereotype, since it meant that society expected me to succeed; I wasn't feeling like anyone expected me to succeed after my miserable time in 8th grade. However, when I gave it more thought, I realized how bad the stereotype was. It put down other minorities by implying that none work harder than Asians. And it labeled me as something I wasn't: a focused overachiever who doesn't rock the boat.

Learning about the model minority stereotype made me realize why so many Asians I knew were stressed about grades. The book helped me think about the expectations I was resisting at school and at home; it was like people assumed I would get good grades and be obedient just because I was Asian—not because I was Jordan. It made me angry at the stereotype, and a little less angry at myself.

Still, I entered high school with the same rebellious attitude I'd had through junior high. I was loud and obnoxious in my classes and was almost suspended for throwing a book at my freshman year global history teacher (though really I was passing it to its owner across the room—through the air). Even though I avoided suspension, I was still doing badly in school.

Around that time, I was diagnosed with a mild case of attention deficit disorder (ADD); it's a learning problem that causes the person who has it to be easily distracted, and makes it harder for him or her to concentrate. Finding out about my ADD made me feel like I stood out even more, especially since I was Asian. How stereotypically Asian could I be when I had to take medication just to sit quietly in class and learn?

But the medication helped me focus, and I didn't feel the same impulse to blurt out wise-ass comments in class. I felt more in control, and in a way, that made me less angry.

Since I wasn't as obnoxious in class, things got cooler with my classmates. Even though I wasn't the model minority child my parents wanted me to be—and I was still mad at them for expecting me to be that way—I wasn't feeling so badly about myself.

After freshman year, my parents lowered their standards for me. They accept that I'm going down my own path—which does include college, even if it's not the Ivy League as my mom was hoping. Things are calmer at home, which is a relief.

I've also found the group of people I'm comfortable around, who happen to be mostly black and Hispanic. I do have Asian and white friends, but race isn't an issue for me in making friends; it's about personality. Two of my best friends—Ian and Ptah, who are black—were more focused than I was about school, which was a good influence on me when I was angry over yet another failed test.

I related to them because they know how to balance doing well in school with being able to get down, chill, and party on the side. I didn't have to choose between the total rebel or the total goody two-shoes. I could be a balance of both, which I think is how I naturally am.

Ptah told me once that he thinks the stereotypes Asians have to deal with aren't bad. He feels the stereotypes blacks are subjected to, like being thugs and drug dealers, are much worse. I understand his point of view. But I still don't like being boxed in by a list of assumptions that don't fit me, which is what the model minority stereotype of Asians does.

The problem with any stereotype is that it gets in the way of people seeing you as an individual. Stereotypes are like an outside skin that people should learn to see past. People are deep and complex. Everyone has a story to tell, something different to say. Everyone wants recognition, and labeling people with stereotypes makes the individual disappear.

When people say stuff to me about Asians being good at math or Asians being quiet, I tell them my experience. Sometimes, though, I just let it slide because I don't feel like arguing. In some ways, I feel like I've escaped the stereotype. I'm happier being myself, kicking it with people who accept me for who I am.

It's funny how easy it is to stereotype each other when most of us want to be seen as the individuals we are. I'm Jordan: The loud, obnoxious, college-bound Asian-American kid from Flushing, Queens, who has something to say.

Jordan was 17 when he wrote this story. He went on to college at SUNY New Paltz, majoring in public relations.

Chinese Parents, American Me

By Ngan-Fong Huang

About a year ago, I bought a pair of baggy jeans and a long shirt that I buttoned only at the top. When my mom saw my new outfit, she shouted, "Look at your jeans! They're too wide and too long for you." I just stared at her, shocked by her reaction.

"They're sagging from your waist and scraping on the ground," she continued. "What are you trying to be? Like those gangsters whose jeans hang so low that they nearly fall to the ground?"

About a week later I tried the jeans on again and noticed that they seemed a lot shorter. I immediately looked at the hemline and saw strands of blue thread sticking out. I realized that my mom had secretly snuck into my room, searched my closet for the jeans, cut a few inches off the bottoms, and then sewed them back up. I was furious. I stormed into her room and asked, "Why did you cut off the bottoms of my jeans? They were mine! How could you do this without asking me?"

"I told you they were too long," was all she said.

"Now I'll never wear these jeans again!" I yelled. "I'll get new ones."

You can call me the typical American-born Chinese (ABC). Like most immigrants, my parents came here for a better future—for themselves and for my sisters and me. But I often feel torn between the ways of my parents and those of the society in which I grew up. On one hand, I want to be accepted by my friends as an American. On the other hand, my parents want me to maintain our traditions. Not knowing what to do, I try to find a middle ground.

"We don't celebrate Christmas," I said. My friend looked shocked.

When I was little, I was comfortable thinking of myself only as Chinese. I had always been sheltered by my family and had not had much contact with other cultures. It was only in kindergarten that I began opening my eyes to all the different people around me.

Because there were no other Chinese families in the neighborhood, all my friends were either Hispanic or African-American. They could not speak Chinese, did not know what the Moon Festival was, or even about the days when we honor our deceased ancestors. I felt very lonely being the only Asian.

I wanted to be accepted. I wanted to be just like my friends. So I did the only logical thing I could do—I too began to idolize Bugs Bunny and Big Bird. I played with the same kinds of Barbie dolls, and played yard games like tag and hopscotch, just like they did. And my friends finally began to accept me. But no matter how I tried to fit in, I always knew I was different from them. I was not a true American. My straight, dark brown hair and almond-shaped eyes looked different from my friends' light, curly hair and large, round eyes. My eyelashes didn't curl up the way theirs did either.

That December, one of my friends asked me, "What presents are you getting from Santa this year?" I was confused. Earlier in the year I had heard my friends talk about a jolly, white-bearded Santa who flew into the air with reindeer, but my parents had never mentioned him before. As far as I knew, Chinese New Year was the most festive occasion of the year, not Christmas. I didn't know how to respond but finally answered, "No, we don't celebrate Christmas." My friend looked shocked, as if I was the most deprived child in the world.

Growing up, television sitcoms made me feel even more like I was not a real American. By the time I was 8 years old, I could already see how the children in the television shows had such open relationships with their parents. They could ask them for advice about anything—school, even boyfriends. The teenagers were free to stay out late, could dress however they wanted, and were not pressured to get good grades. Best of all, the family members always hugged and forgave each other.

That was not how my family was. There were no hugs or any signs of affection at all. For us it was just supposed to be inferred. And even now, at the age of 17, I would never even think about talking to either of my parents about dating because I know they do not approve of it at this age. Life in my family is more about school and grades, not relationships. My parents also think that girls should dress conservatively—no miniskirts, tank tops, or other clothing that shows more skin than just the arms, face, and legs below the knees.

Often I feel confused because I can't decide whether to go on obeying my parents or do what I feel is right for me. I've tried to make my parents see that I'm mature enough to control my own life. They may be upset and nag me for coming home later than 7 p.m., for example. But I try to convince them that it's OK because I was at the library or doing something else important. I know that eventually they will get used to the idea.

I am not the first one in my family to face difficulties trying to open up their traditional thinking. My older sisters were the first rebels who fought to Americanize my parents' ways. While fighting for their own rights, they also paved the way for the privileges I have now, such as staying out until 8 p.m. and being allowed to go out with friends.

My older sisters have taught me a great deal about what my parents expect of me—particularly concerning boys. Although my sisters always understood the value of education, they could not resist having secret boyfriends. My eldest sister, Jane, had her first boyfriend when she was just 16—not only that, but he was Vietnamese. When my parents found out, the house became a war zone. They resented the idea of a boyfriend, especially one that was not Chinese. Every night the living room was filled with loud arguments in Chinese and never-ending cries.

I accept myself as a Chinese-American, meaning that I follow ways of both cultures.

"Stop controlling my life," my sister would scream. "It's not for you to decide."

"If you are under my roof, you'd better listen to me," my parents would yell back. "You shouldn't be distracted from school by boys."

"Fine, I'll move out of the house," my sister said.

My parents had nothing more to threaten her with, except, "You'll never come back under this roof if you're so disobedient. We're not paying for your college tuition."

Jane did end up moving out, not caring about school or her college education. Eventually, she broke away from her Vietnamese boyfriend and made up with my parents, but she never did go to college and now works as a beautician. Jane's experience established the idea that my other sister and I could not have close relationships, especially with guys who were not Chinese. My parents try to divert our attention away from guys by emphasizing the importance of education.

It is the goal of many Chinese parents to have children who are highly educated and prominent in society. My parents think that if my second sister, now a business major, had not had relationships in high school, she would have entered what they consider a more prominent profession, like law or medicine.

They have accepted my interest in science and medicine and want me to be a doctor. Luckily, that's my goal as well, so I probably won't cause a family disturbance. But if I decide to pursue other areas, like interior decorating or broadcast journalism, I am sure my parents would object.

Meanwhile, my parents urge us all to retain the customs, language, and beliefs of our culture. Last Halloween when I came home from school with neon pink hair, my mom was outraged. "You're looking like one of those gangsters," she said.

"But it's temporary," I told her. "It'll wash off easily in water."

"You'd better not put anything else in your hair again," was all she said after she finished personally washing the dye out of my hair. To my mother, and probably for many other traditional parents, hair color should be natural—in the case of the Chinese, dark brown or black. I was furious at how closed-minded my mom was. "Ma," I said, "my friends can do whatever they want to their hair and their parents don't mind."

She glared at me and said, "I don't care what those parents think. Just don't be like them."

As much as I would like to dye my hair, stay out late, not worry about school, and have boyfriends the way my American friends do, I understand that there are valid reasons to follow many aspects of the Chinese culture. I think one reason my parents don't want me and my siblings to date is because they're afraid we may end up marrying a non-Chinese person and losing our culture.

While the more American side of me becomes angry at the thought of only being allowed to marry another Chinese person, my Chinese side is learning to respect this restriction. In the past

I might have thought that my parents were only trying to be cruel, but I now understand their reasons. Since they only speak minimal English, in order to have a healthy relationship with their sons- or daughters-in-law, it is logical that they should be able to communicate with them. More importantly, our Chinese culture is already being lost in the United States. Prohibiting interracial or interethnic marriage is their attempt to hold on to our language and traditions.

These days, I accept myself as a Chinese-American, meaning that I follow ways of both cultures. In some ways I am more American, like in the way I dress. And I am the one who chooses who my friends are—whether my parents approve or not. After all, I am 17 and capable of leading my own life. But in other areas, I still accept some of the more traditional ways, such the idea that I shouldn't marry outside my race.

Slowly, my parents and I are making progress in compromising with each other. A week after my mom cut those baggy jeans, for instance, I went out and bought another pair. This time, however, they were a little shorter; my parents didn't complain about it, and I didn't mind the jeans the way they were. My parents can regulate my life to an extent for now, but ultimately I know I will be the one to decide what my future will look like.

Ngan-Fong was 16 when she wrote this story.
She later went to college and became an engineer.

Gabriel Pinto

Tongue-Tied

By Amy Huang

"Awww, man," I thought to myself as my cousin Lin handed me my vocabulary list of the day: table, fish, supermarket. But I picked up my pencil and started copying the words. That's what I did every weekend of 4th grade and the summer after.

When I was 9, my family moved to the U.S. from China. I didn't know any English, but because of my age, I was put into 4th grade. I was scared; I didn't even know the alphabet! My other cousin, who spoke English, asked the school officials to put me in a lower grade, but they refused.

So I was relieved to meet three American-born Chinese girls in my class: Sue, Linda, and Marie. They were the only ones I could communicate with because they spoke Chinese. So the teacher told them to show me around the school and help me adjust. Nobody else in my class cared to talk to me or be friendly.

I felt unwelcome, but I wasn't surprised. I mean, why would anyone talk to a stranger who can't speak the language? Why help someone learn? Linda, Sue, and Marie seemed nice at first. I felt good being able to speak to kids from the same culture because it made me feel like I fit in and had friends.

A few weeks later, though, I found out that they made fun of me behind my back. I was sitting next to Sue when I saw her writing a letter to her friend, telling her how she hated me and how stupid I was. Although I couldn't read English well, I knew enough to figure out what she wrote. I felt betrayed because I thought she was my friend. Then it got worse. Sue called me "Sei chuen," which is like a Chinese version of dumb, right to my face. And several times, Linda deliberately spilled water on me from her water bottle.

People from my own culture had turned against me. It felt like being smacked across the face by my own hand.

That made me angry. I wanted to tell the teacher to get Linda in trouble, but I had no idea how to express myself. I had no choice but to try to avoid her.

What really made me upset was what they did to me during recess. Sometimes Sue, Linda, and Marie would come up to me with three other Chinese-American friends. One of them would sneak up behind me and grab my hat. Then they'd run around and toss my hat from one person to another to keep it away from me. The torture didn't stop until the end of recess. I felt I was like playing monkey in the middle with enemies that I couldn't beat.

All I did was weakly tell them in Chinese, "Give it back." I was frustrated because I couldn't do anything else and I didn't have anyone there to help me. Worse, I felt betrayed and disappointed because people from my own culture had turned against me. It felt like being smacked across the face by my own hand. I wanted to cry, but I didn't. I refused to give them the satisfaction of knowing that they'd hurt me.

I wondered why they had to pick on me. Maybe they thought it was fun to pick on a new kid, or maybe they felt superior to me because they were "Americans" and I was a foreigner. I hated myself for not being able to speak English—I couldn't do anything about my bullies since I couldn't communicate with the teacher. I didn't even try to say anything to my teacher because I thought, "What chance do I have against Sue, Linda, and Marie, who can speak English and would probably deny everything I'd say?"

I tried telling my parents about it, but that was like going to a dentist when I have a stomachache. "Just tell them to stop bothering you and stay away from them," they advised. I thought to myself, "Yeah, right, like they'll do what I say." So I was forced to put up with their bullying the rest of the year.

That summer, though, I worked hard to learn English. Every day, I memorized new vocabulary words and my cousin quizzed me. As I built my vocabulary, I asked my cousin to speak English around me, instead of Chinese. A few weeks later, I was able to talk to her in English.

When I entered 5th grade, I was able to express myself and make friends, which made me feel more American. I felt like I was fitting in. I was a lot happier. And fortunately, none of my tormentors were in my class.

I also progressed in school. In 4th grade, when I was still struggling with the language, I was unable to complete my classwork and homework. Since I couldn't understand my teacher, I paid no attention to what she said. But in 5th grade, I found myself listening carefully to my teacher's words. I did my homework every night and had a strong desire to achieve. I found myself going to the library and opening a new world as I borrowed and read books.

Reading those books improved my reading skills and introduced me to American culture. I learned that Americans are into sports like baseball and football. American kids hang out at parks, movie theaters, and pizzerias. I found myself being slowly absorbed into American culture, watching baseball and eating hamburgers and hot dogs. I liked becoming Americanized. It led me to make friends outside of my own background.

The memory of being bullied became distant. But because of what I went through in 4th grade, I told myself, "I will never make fun of anyone who can't speak English." Since then, if my friends make a comment about a person who can't speak the language well, I ignore them and try to change the subject.

Ironically, however, I can't help but sometimes feel annoyed at my own family members who can't speak English. Every month, when the bills arrive, I have to explain to my mom or dad what they say. I often get frustrated because I'm not very good at translating business terms like "interest" or "suspension" into Chinese, and my parents seem unable to understand what I'm saying.

I told myself, "I will never make fun of anyone who can't speak English."

"Shame on you! How can you not know how to translate after all these years you have been to school?" my parents yell when I can't give them a full translation.

"Going to school doesn't mean that I know everything," I say angrily.

A few months ago, my dad asked me to help him prepare for his naturalization exam. I didn't like doing it because I had to repeat myself many, many times before he managed to understand or memorize what I'd said.

"How do you read this question?" my dad asked.

"It says 'Who wrote The Star Spangled Banner?'" I said.

"What? Say that again. Say it slower," he said.

"Who... wrote... The... Star... Spangled... Banner?" I repeated.

"Who wrote deh sta spangul banner?" my dad repeated.

"No dad, it's 'Star Spangled Banner,'" I said with gritted teeth.

"Star Spangled Banner," he repeated again.

"Yes, that's it," I said.

"What is it again?" he asked.

I was really annoyed and angry because I couldn't understand why he was so slow in understanding me. My mom noticed how impatient I was and got extremely upset with me. Not for the first time, she gave me a lecture on being nice and helping people. "Don't think you're better than others just because you know some English," she scolded. "You needed help getting where you are too."

But I felt guilty even without my mother's scolding. I feel really bad when I look back on that moment because I should've been more understanding. I am impatient and find it hard to stay calm when I'm asked to repeat the same thing over and over again, even though the way I learned English was through constant repetition. I should've thought about how much harder it was for my dad to learn English than me, because he's a lot older and he doesn't go to school.

I'm hoping that, next time, when I'm asked to explain something to someone who can't understand English, I'll be more patient and less irritated. It's hard to control emotions, but I'll try. I was helpless once myself and know how awful it felt.

Amy was 15 when she wrote this story.

My Life as an ABC

By Victoria Law

When I was younger, my parents wanted me to become more Americanized. In nursery school, the teachers complained that they couldn't understand my English with its Chinese accent, picked up from my Chinese-born parents, so my father took it upon himself to teach me proper English, like Professor Higgins in *My Fair Lady*.

My dad's English wasn't perfect either, but he seemed to think it was. (He'd gone to college in the United States and had become a U.S. citizen.) Instead of letting me go out to play with other kids, he made me sit and study lists of English words that he put together. I would have to read the lists aloud until he thought I could pronounce all the words perfectly.

Throughout my childhood, my parents did a series of things that distanced me from my Chinese heritage and culture.

First, they discouraged me from speaking the language. When I was very young I learned enough Chinese at home to carry on a rough conversation. But once I started school, my parents stopped speaking Chinese to me. They used it only when they wanted to have a private conversation, and didn't want me to know what they were saying.

For example, one day when my father was bad-mouthing the neighbors, I exclaimed, "I know what you're saying!" My father told me that I misunderstood, that he had said that the neighbors were good, kind people. I don't think my parents realized that they were cutting me off from learning Chinese.

When I was 2, my parents moved from a Chinese community to a neighborhood with almost no Chinese people. When I started school, they sent me to a nearby private school which was mostly white. During the summer, I was sent to mostly white summer camps. The few Chinese kids I met were as Americanized as I was, so I never minded not being able to speak or understand Chinese.

My parents never guessed that over the years I would come to feel more American than Chinese.

I grew up without feeling that anything was missing from my identity: my ethnicity was never an issue in elementary school except on rare occasions when someone teased me by making a racial slur. At home, my father would sometimes mention sending me to Chinese school, but he did it mostly to annoy me with the threat of having even more school to go to; he was never serious about it.

My parents never guessed that over the years I would come to feel more American than Chinese and resist all attempts to be put more in touch with my Chinese heritage and culture. If they'd known, they might have done things differently.

It wasn't until I was 13 that they started making an effort to connect me to my roots. Instead of sending me to camp, my father started taking me to Hong Kong for a couple of weeks every summer to visit relatives. For the first time, I felt self-conscious about not speaking Chinese because everyone (my relatives, the shopkeepers, the waiters) expected me to.

I could communicate with my relatives to varying degrees, depending on how much English education they'd received. I had no problem talking to my grandmother because she visits the U.S. every two years and is fluent in English. With others, it was more difficult. When strangers realized that I couldn't speak Chinese, they didn't even bother to conceal the disdain they felt for me, muttering things under their breath that probably would have translated to, "Stupid American, forgetting her culture."

My relatives initially went on and on about how I should learn Chinese, but eventually they stopped. I think they gradually realized that I had no interest in it and would remain more American than Chinese, but I doubt they approved. Occasionally they still mentioned something about how nice it would be if I could speak Chinese.

It was only after starting high school that I began to realize how much my American upbringing had left me without any awareness of my Chinese heritage. Studying European and American history at school, I began to realize that I wasn't white like other kids. I didn't share a common past with them. But I didn't fit in with other Chinese people either.

At the neighborhood pool hall and park I made friends with some Chinese people in their early twenties. They were amazed that I knew no Chinese at all. Most of them had immigrated from Hong Kong only a few years before and spoke English with thick accents. I felt left out whenever they spoke Chinese, which was often. Sometimes, one of the girls would say that I should learn. Or some of the guys would tease me for being ABC (American-Born Chinese). But I felt that if I had asked them to teach me, they would have made fun of me more.

It wasn't only the language that made me feel different from them. There was also a cultural difference. They were more submissive. They never complained about the way their parents treated them, even if they were unreasonably strict or abusive. One girl told me that her father had once tied her to a bathroom pipe to punish her, but then defended him by saying that it was to protect her from becoming a "bad person."

The girls accepted that their boyfriends lied to or cheated on them, constantly forgiving them and taking them back. It made me angry that they seemed to perpetuate the stereotype of Asian women as passive and submissive. I think our conflicts about values just reinforced their view that I was more American than Chinese.

When strangers realized that I couldn't speak Chinese, they didn't even bother to conceal the disdain they felt for me.

When I was in 11th grade, I transferred from private school to a public school where there were many Asians (both new immigrants and American-born) who weren't as assimilated as I was. They were amazed that I was more American than Chinese.

I think both my teachers and the other Chinese students were used to a more stereotypical Chinese person—quiet, studious, and good in math and science—not an outgoing girl with black lipstick and oversized combat boots who constantly had a non-school-related book in her hand and whose mathematical talent consisted of memorizing telephone numbers.

Some of the Chinese students teased me. Once, a girl asked me if I had ever considered going to Chinese school on Saturdays to learn the language. When her friend pointed out that she didn't go, she smiled and said, "That's because I'm not an ABC." I don't think she meant to make me feel inferior, but I felt that she was insulting me by using that derogatory term.

More and more, I felt that I had lost touch with my heritage. On the streets, I'd be approached by elderly Chinese women who most likely needed directions. I could only shrug my shoulders and say, "Don't know," the only Chinese phrase I know. They would simply look at me and walk away. I'd feel awful both about not being able to help them and not knowing the language.

I started wanting to learn Chinese and learn more about my culture. I began going to see Chinese films like *The Blue Kite,* a film about a family in Communist China from 1953 through the Cultural Revolution in the 1960s, which was banned in China because of its politics. The film showed how brutal life in China has been under Communist rule.

And, although I'd read Chinese-American authors like Maxine Hong Kingston and Amy Tan, I'd never really delved into the actual history. I started to read about the government's massacre of student activists at Tiananmen Square and also started clipping articles on China and Hong Kong from magazines and newspapers, trying to stay up-to-date on everything going on there. I hope to visit China someday and get a feel for life there (and maybe spark the next revolution).

I still can't speak Chinese except for a few simple words. But I plan to minor in Chinese in college and hope to become fluent. I'm tired of feeling that I don't belong to any race since I'm neither an all-American white girl nor a submissive Chinese girl. I'm sick of feeling defensive whenever someone asks me about my heritage or the Chinese language. I want to change that.

Although I don't see myself embracing values that I consider medieval and outdated, I want to be more in touch with my Asian side. I want to feel that I could fit into a Chinese community. After all, that is also my heritage. I don't think of it as losing or rejecting my American side, but I want to feel like a whole person, not someone who's missing a part of herself.

Victoria was 17 when she wrote this story. She later graduated from college and became an activist, writer, and photographer in New York City.

Ignoring the Stares

By Leneli Liggayu

I met Jeremy on my first day of high school in my 7th period leadership class. Eventually I gave him my number because he liked my friend and wanted some tips on how to approach her. But in the end, he diverted most of his attention to me. As the school year went on, he asked me out countless times. I kept telling him I wasn't ready to have a boyfriend. But as we began to hang out more, I found that I liked his dorky but cute sense of humor.

When we watched a movie or TV show, he'd laugh at jokes that no one else thought were funny. I liked that he had goals—he wanted to become a musician and was passionate about playing the guitar instead of wasting his time on video games. Those were the things that defined him to me, not the fact that he happened to be black.

When I realized I liked Jeremy, I was afraid of what my parents would say. I'd never approached them about the subject of interracial dating because they didn't want me to have a boyfriend at all, let alone one who wasn't Filipino like us. But I imagined them not accepting Jeremy. After all, that's what happened in the movies.

When I was 11, I saw *Save the Last Dance,* a movie about a white girl dating a black boy despite opposition from family and friends. I also remember when *Monster's Ball* came out, a movie about a white prison guard who finds company in an executed prisoner's black wife. Both movies suggested that many people didn't approve of interracial dating. I started to think maybe interracial dating was bad.

At the time, I didn't know any Filipinos who dated outside our ethnicity. I assumed that when I got older, I'd meet a nice Filipino boy whom my parents would adore and who would meet all my standards. But my first boyfriend didn't turn out to be the person I expected.

Two years after we met, the summer before my junior year, Jeremy's persistence finally paid off. I invited him to a birthday party I was throwing for a friend. As he was leaving, he kissed me goodnight, and we made it official the next day—we were a couple. When Jeremy wanted to introduce me to his parents one month into the relationship, it felt like a big step after such a short time. I thought about how much easier it was for couples from the same background. When they brought their girlfriend or boyfriend home to their parents, it wouldn't be as big a shock as I imagined I would be to Jeremy's parents.

My parents didn't want me to have a boyfriend at all, let alone one who wasn't Filipino like us.

Jeremy had met my parents only once, at a school concert before we'd started dating. When I told them we were dating, they didn't react irrationally like I'd imagined. They just said, "OK." I guess they figured that I was growing up. They've never asked about him, not even now, but I think that's because they're uncomfortable with me having a boyfriend of any race.

The day I went to meet Jeremy's parents, I met him at a bus terminal near his house. I wore a white skirt and purple blouse, and in my hand was a plastic container with strawberry shortcake inside. I wanted to make a good first impression. It felt strange to walk through the bus terminal in my girly get-up, which only drew more attention to me, a Filipina girl alone in a mostly black and Latino area. Heads turned and eyebrows raised. When Jeremy came up behind me and tickled my sides, I could almost feel the stares burning into my back.

When we got to his house, I sat on the couch and waited nervously while Jeremy ran upstairs to see if his mom was ready. I stood up quickly when he came back down. "She wants to meet you," he said. I slowly followed him past the kitchen and up the creaky stairs. I walked into his mom's bedroom, holding the cake out like a present, and time seemed to stand still. There was Jeremy's mom, sitting on the bed with a huge smile on her face. "Jeremy, you didn't tell me she was so pretty!" she said.

I blushed, laughed nervously, and extended my hand. She took it. "Hi, I'm Leneli. It's really nice to meet you," I said, handing her the cake. "I brought this for you."

She gasped in surprise and grinned from ear to ear. "Thank you! Jeremy's father and I love strawberry shortcake."

She told me she was pleased to see that her son had found himself a good girl. I was blushing the whole time.

"She loves you!" Jeremy said excitedly after she left. I sighed with relief. Since then, I talk to his mom almost every week for a few minutes when I'm on the phone with Jeremy.

Since Jeremy's parents accepted us, I was hoping the rest of world would, too. Maybe interracial dating was no longer a big deal, after all. But when we went to the movies or the park, I still got the feeling that people were looking at us. Jeremy never seemed to notice, though. I began to wonder if I was imagining these things because I felt weird about it myself. I was always worried that something might happen—a confrontation, an offense.

One day Jeremy and I were at his house and we decided to

go to a mall across town. We got our wallets and cell phones and headed toward the bus stop. We decided to take a shortcut through a tiny local mall. When the automatic doors opened, I felt all eyes on me. People were looking at us as if to say, "Why's he with her?" As usual, Jeremy didn't seem to notice.

We jogged across the parking lot and past a park, where a few little girls stopped playing and began to whisper to each other while pointing at me. Was I imagining all of this? I still don't know. When the bus came five minutes later, I still sensed that I was the only Asian person for miles. I started worrying about racial slurs that might be thrown at me, like "ch-nk" and "dog-eater," which I'd heard in my own neighborhood before.

I started worrying about racial slurs that might be thrown at me, like "ch-nk" and "dog-eater."

I never told Jeremy what I'd felt at the mall. I didn't want him to think I was overreacting. But as I was writing this story, I began to question why we'd never discussed the fact that we were an interracial couple. It was the only territory we'd never covered in conversation. I was nervous about bringing it up because it didn't seem to faze Jeremy and I didn't want him to think I was making a big deal out of nothing. But recently I decided to sit down with him to talk about it.

Jeremy told me that even before we started dating, race hadn't been an issue to him. He said dating is simply what happens between people who are interested in each other, no matter what their backgrounds. I asked him what he thought about interracial relationships now that he was in one. He said it still wasn't an issue for him, but he realizes now that fewer people are open to the idea than he'd imagined. And it turned out he did notice when people would give us critical looks. He just chose to ignore them.

It had taken me so long to bring up the subject that I felt silly when I heard his thoughts on it. I felt better knowing that I hadn't been paranoid about people's reactions, because he'd seen them all, too. Since then, I've started using Jeremy's approach. Whenever we get the odd stare, I ignore it.

I know interracial dating is still an issue to some people, but Jeremy and I refuse to let it get to us. We go to restaurants and ignore the few stares we get. We hold hands walking through the mall. We take the stupid things some people say about us and turn it into a good laugh—like when someone told me that I'd be better off with a Filipino because blacks and Asians "just don't work." When I told Jeremy that, we laughed because we obviously "work" and have been working for a long time.

Jeremy and I have been together for more than two years now and our relationship is stronger than ever. What we have is truthful and unbiased and that's what love should be.

Leneli was 16 when she wrote this story. She completed high school and went to college, majoring in journalism.

William Pope

Where Nobody Knows My Name

By Sung Park

Whoosh, whoosh! My neighbors are playing basketball again... at 1 in the morning. It's just my luck that I get stuck next door to these people who think that playing sports at all hours of the day is normal.

My neighbors are the Arnolds. That is not their real last name. I don't know their real name, so I nicknamed them the Arnolds. They live next door to me and have for the last seven years. Aside from their odd basketball-playing hours, I don't know much about them. No one knows each other here. Correction—my family does not know anyone here. Maybe it's because we don't fit in. After all, we must be the only Asian people within a one-mile radius.

Everyone is basically white and Jewish, but my family

doesn't mind. We're content with just living here, particularly my dad. He was proud that we were able to move to a "white" neighborhood, that we would no longer have to be grouped with all the other Asians who live in a cluster in a nearby neighborhood—where we used to live.

When we moved to our new neighborhood, we did everything we could to get to know our neighbors. We tried to be friendly and hoped that our family would fit in. I remember my father inviting the people across the street to our house for Easter dinner. And for Labor Day. And Thanksgiving. They never accepted. They never even gave us an explanation. "Something to do," was mumbled into our ears as they continued washing their white BMWs. (It seems like the only kinds of cars people own in my area are BMWs or Mercedes. We have a 7-year-old blue Volvo.)

Our neighbors invited themselves over to each other's houses almost every week and even went on vacations together. My family wasn't asking to spend a week at a resort with them, but knowing their names would have been nice. I guess my family didn't know when to quit, especially my dad. No matter how rude our neighbors were, he kept on talking to them, waving and yelling, "Good morning!" to the people across the street. They'd just keep watering their lawns, eyes downcast.

No matter how rude our neighbors were, my dad kept on talking to them, waving and yelling, "Good morning!"

One summer a few years back, my family planted some tomatoes in our backyard. The plants exploded with tomatoes at the end of the summer and we had more than we knew what to do with. My parents filled a basket with them, and I mean it was big—they had a hard time carrying it out the door. They casually sauntered over to the Arnolds and offered them some of our "harvest." The Arnolds just gave them a look that said, "We wouldn't touch that stuff with a 10-foot pole."

My dad looked sort of depressed and upset. He was offering an olive branch to our neighbors and they were nothing but ungrateful, prejudiced people. I started to get really steamed. I mean, who did they think they were to treat us like we were criminals? Just because our eyes slant down and our skin is a shade more yellow than theirs?

You may be thinking, "Big deal, ignoring people is not a crime." It's not as though they were beating us to death or throwing garbage at us. But when you see everyone around you being friendly with each other and barely giving you a nod of acknowledgement, it's hard not to be bitter about it.

Still, in spite of the way our neighbors have treated us, I can't stand the idea of leaving this neighborhood. It's very pretty. Small, quaint houses are on lots lined with either white picket fences or sturdy black metal ones. In the southern part of the neighborhood, the houses are at least 100 years old, although some are newly renovated. The old blends in with the new and all the houses are tasteful, not tacky-looking.

The streets are made of paving stones, not asphalt. There is a bridge that connects one apartment building to another and the architecture is very old-fashioned. It's got greenery and big bushes dotted with small rosettes in the spring, and there are little pots of Swedish Ivy on every corner. In the winter, the terrain is perfect for sledding. It reminds me of the New England scenery I see on postcards.

The neighborhood is also very safe compared to other places I could be living—no burglaries or drug addicts hanging out on street corners. I don't have to worry about getting mugged, like I would in many of the neighborhoods where Asian immigrants live.

Even if it wasn't dangerous, I don't think that I would be happy living in an all-Asian neighborhood. I don't speak Korean, so I wouldn't be able to mix with a lot of recent immigrants. And I don't really want to be grouped with the Asians who struggle and are considered a minority. I never considered myself as anything but a regular person and never gave a thought to my race until we moved here. I had never encountered racism before.

But because I like other things about the neighborhood so much, I try to ignore the hostility around me and just keep to myself. I hope I'm not encouraging racism by not expressing my feelings to my neighbors, but I don't know any other way to deal with the discrimination. I doubt they would admit what they're doing if I spoke to them about it, anyway.

When I become an adult and get a place of my own, I hope that there will not be as much racism, but as long as it doesn't get violent or vindictive, I'll let sleeping dogs lie. Hopefully, I won't have to experience discrimination and prejudice in the future. But at least, if I did, I know now that I could live with it. I have for the past seven years.

It's sad to think people won't let my family and me into their lives just because we're Korean. Since I moved here, I feel like I've become jaded, as if it's aged me 50 years. And I can't help getting a chill down my spine sometimes as I'm walking down my block. The houses are unwelcoming and I feel a bitter hostility surrounding me. I'm reminded of it every day. I saw a row of tidy bright yellow tulips in a neighbor's front yard on a clear blue afternoon. I wondered, "How can a person grow delicate flowers with such loving care and give my family the cold shoulder all the time?"

It's sad to think people won't let my family and me into their lives just because we're Korean.

Sung was in high school when she wrote this story.

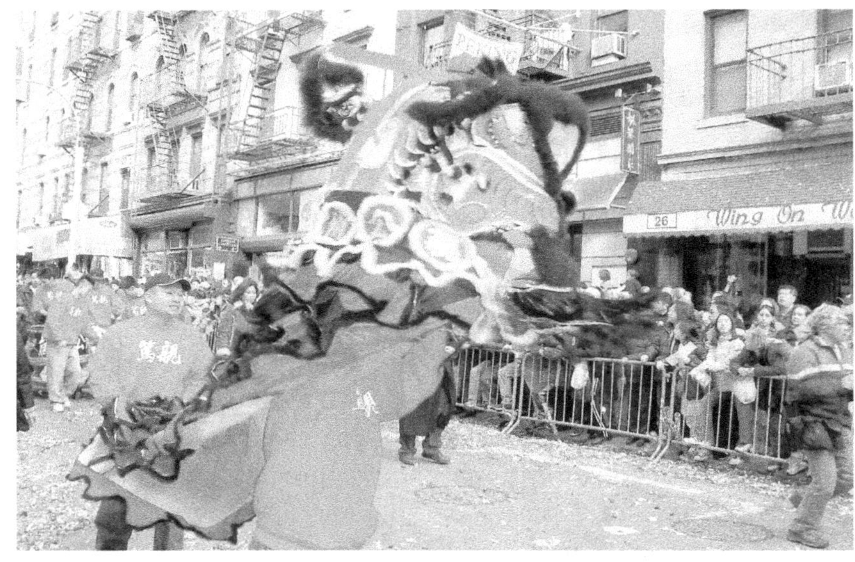

YC Art Dept.

Beyond the Great Wall of Chinatown

By Xiao Ling Zhong

Like many Chinese immigrants, my family and I have lived in Chinatown since the day we arrived in this country. We had to adjust to a new world, and I had to go to school without knowing a word of English. The seven hours of the school day felt as long as a year, and I glanced at my watch several times each minute. But when I went back to my neighborhood and received its hug, a long day's fear, sadness, and loneliness were gone.

Living in Chinatown is not like living in China. In my building, I know only two families. I haven't been to their apartments, nor do I ask them for anything. I only exchange a few words when we meet each other on the stairway. In other words, we are strangers.

Back in China, I lived in a little village. I knew almost everybody. I visited their houses, played with them. We even ate together. The whole village was like an extended family. The elders told me stories, taught me life lessons, and trusted me to do things for them. The children were like brothers and sisters.

Still, living in Chinatown reminds me of my first home in China. It helps me to preserve my cultural identity and makes me proud to have Chinese values, like respecting my elders and not bragging or boasting, which have passed from generation to generation for thousands of years. I am glad to live in Chinatown. But in some ways, the neighborhood also holds me back. It isolates me.

I've lived in New York now for four years, and I still stick to my own kind of people. If my family had moved into an integrated area, I would speak English more fluently and I would have more friends from other parts of the world. I would learn about their traditions, cultures, and attitudes. And maybe I would feel at home in this multicultural country.

I feel like I'm living in a hole deep underground, seeing only a very tiny portion of the beautiful sky.

I might become more self-confident, like so many of the Americans I see. In my English class, American students always express their opinions and disagree with other people's ideas, but most of my Chinese friends and I hardly raise our hands. Part of it is a language problem, but I also think that in my culture, we're taught not to say what we think.

But right now, the only place I really feel at home in New York is in Chinatown. Sometimes I feel like I am living in a hole deep underground, seeing only a very tiny portion of the beautiful sky, and have no idea about the other parts of the boundless universe. I know the sky is wide and beautiful. I'd like to fly out and take a look.

A typical day in Chinatown is noisy and swarming. For me this is a good thing. Being in the crowds in Chinatown gives me a feeling of warmth and closeness. After 6 p.m., the streets become active, probably the noisiest moment of the day. Everyone leaves work and goes shopping for the night's meal. On the crowded streets, there are fish markets, fruit stalls, and vegetable booths. Peddlers yell to attract customers' attention, saying things like, "Very pretty and fresh tomatoes, one dollar for two pounds, hurry up and buy."

Customers bargain with sellers about the prices. Sometimes some non-Chinese people come by, looking curiously at vegetables they have never seen before, and asking how to cook them. I go from stall to stall, comparing the prices and the quality of the food and fruits. At the end, I am loaded with several packages of vegetables, apples, grapes, oranges, fish, and shrimp.

The hustle and bustle feels familiar and I remember shopping for meals in China. My homesickness is soothed by walking on the streets of this neighborhood, passing all the stalls, and seeing the store signs and street signs that are written in both English and Chinese.

When I finally get home at night, I open the old, dark red door of my five-story building. I walk under the dim light and step forward along the narrow hallway, where two people cannot walk together side by side, for what seems like miles. Then I turn left at the aged wooden stairs, and walk up three flights to the fourth floor. At last I take out my keys, open the door, and I'm home.

In front of me is a room that serves as kitchen and dining room. To the left is one bedroom for my parents, with space enough only for a bed. To the right is the room where my brother and I sleep in bunkbeds. Our room is also the living room for the whole family, and furniture occupies every inch of space. When guests visit, I am often angry that they talk and play in my "bedroom" and I have no privacy.

But when I compare my problems with others, mine seem like nothing. As streams of immigrants come to the United States to pursue their American dreams, crowded Chinatown becomes even more crowded, and many people have to squeeze into small apartments.

My uncle's friend lives downstairs. His family, six adults and one baby, live in an apartment about the same size as mine. My friend Linda's family rents an apartment with three rooms. "Of course we don't have enough space, I have six family members," she says. And there are other problems in Chinatown besides the housing.

After college and medical school, I might come back to work in a hospital in Chinatown to help Chinese people.

In Chinatown, people who don't speak English can still work in restaurants, shops, bakeries, supermarkets, and offices that are Chinese-speaking. But good jobs in Chinatown are scarce. To receive a small paycheck requires long hours of hard work.

My grandfather works in a small restaurant. He works all day long in the kitchen, washes the vegetables, chops the meat, cooks the food. All day he's near the stove, whether it is the cold winter or the hot summer. My grandmother and my mom work in a garment factory. Their boss doesn't pay them by the hour, but based on how much clothing they make. Cent by cent, dollar by dollar, they earn it with their sweat and long hours.

Sometimes during the weekends I have to help my mom. In the factory, my ears are filled with horrible loud noises from the machines that make buttons and iron the clothing. Listening to the radio, chatting with co-workers, and daydreaming are the only things that get me through the hard and repetitive work. Finally, it is 6 o'clock in the evening, and I am released. I am the first one to leave the factory. On my way home, I think, "Oh, my God, if I had to work the rest of my life like this, I don't know what I would do."

I think I might want to leave Chinatown eventually. I see my parents' helpless faces, and I think I need to work hard, do well in college and medical school, and become a successful doctor so I can leave and help them leave, too. But maybe after college and medical school I will come back to work in a hospital in Chinatown to help Chinese people. Despite all the problems, I feel comfortable in Chinatown, and I am glad I live here.

In the future, though, I am going to mix with other people in this society. I will make friends with them, learn from them, and join the American mainstream. I will have to be brave. If this happens, I'm sure I will more easily fit in. But I also worry that I might lose some of my culture. Perhaps I will forget some of my Chinese customs and it will be like an exchange. I will get something I dream of, but I will have to pay with something I love.

Hopefully, I can have both worlds. I will be Chinese at home, but act like an American outside. I will speak Chinese with my family, and English with classmates and coworkers. I will eat Chinese food at home, and pizza outside. I will be a quiet girl at home, but an outgoing person outside. I'm already beginning to practice this.

Now every morning I take the subway train from the Canal Street station in Chinatown to school. As the train leaves the station and heads for the outside world, I feel happy to get through the wall that closes me inside, and a little bit scared to leave this home.

Xiao Ling was in high school when she wrote this story.

Karolina Zaniesienko

'Chinklish'

By Winnie Tang

It was a cold winter morning when I noticed that my friend Randy had broken the code. My friends and I were hanging out on the corner before school when one of them, Darien, said, "Ah cha, hui my ga feh." That's Cantonese for "Indian, go buy coffee." I stared as Randy, who's Indian, not Chinese, walked to the deli and came back with a cup of coffee. "You owe me a dollar, man," he jokingly said to Darien.

For a few seconds, I just stood there with my mouth open. What was Randy doing understanding our language? "How did you know what he was saying?" I asked him. He laughed. "Oh, Shirley taught me," he said. Like me and the rest of my group of friends, Shirley, his girlfriend, is Chinese.

My friends and I use Cantonese, a Chinese language, to communicate things that we don't want other people to know. Some of my friends and I call this language "Chinklish." For example, when we saw an enormously fat dog walk by, and we didn't want to call it fat in front of its owner, we said it was "ho fay," which, translated from Cantonese, means "really fat." Randy laughed at that because he understood what we said. Randy was like an infiltrator, someone who had cracked the code.

My friends and I mostly communicate in English, but we use our Chinese vocabulary as a convenience. Having two languages to use means we can use Chinese words to express something that's harder to get across in English. For example, when I want to say someone is so incredibly dense and doesn't know how to adapt to changes, I'll use just two words in Chinese and call him "say chun," which translates as "dead stupid."

Randy was like an infiltrator, someone who had cracked the code.

There's no set grammar or rules as to how "Chinklish" is spoken. It's basically English with Chinese words. It's like "Spanglish," when Spanish-speaking people incorporate English words into Spanish. Living in America means we all speak English, but part of our heritage still remains with us.

I made most of my Asian friends in high school. At my junior high school, I was one of maybe 10 Asian people. Most of my friends in junior high were white. High school was definitely a new experience. The first time I arrived at my high school, I was overwhelmed by the number of Asian people there.

I gradually gravitated towards a group of Chinese friends, mainly Cantonese people. Most of them, like me, were born here, or else they came here when they were very young. But we all had Chinese-speaking parents and most of us spoke Cantonese at home.

The majority of Chinese-Americans come from the Cantonese-speaking part of China. Cantonese is the language of Guangzhou, formerly Canton, in southeastern China. It's also the dominant language of Hong Kong. Other Chinese in the U.S. may speak Taiwanese if they come from Taiwan, or they may speak Mandarin, the official language of China. But my friends and I generally think of Cantonese as Chinese.

I think I hang out with mostly Chinese kids because language is a thing we share. We've adapted to an American lifestyle while keeping our Chinese culture. I don't mind having to explain myself and my culture to other people, but it's just so much easier when I don't have to. It's not that my friends and I don't want to be friends with other people, but language represents our culture. It's a link between us. By speaking "Chinklish," we're keeping our culture as first generation Americans.

But my friends and I are careful about using "Chinklish" too much. If we did, then it might seem like we didn't know English, and we had to resort to using Chinese. We don't want to come across as "fobby," as in "fresh off the boat." That's a derogatory term which I admit some Chinese people use to describe recent immigrants who can't speak English.

It seems hypocritical for those of us who are Chinese to discriminate against them, but recent Chinese immigrants aren't like us. They dress differently, act differently, and most important of all, talk differently. At my high school, the new immigrants hang out with their own groups, and we hang out with ours. We're Chinese, but we're American, too.

By speaking "Chinklish," we're keeping our culture as first generation Americans.

But while there's not a lot of mixing among the groups, once in a while, a non-Chinese person will hang out with a group of Chinese people. In Randy's case, he chilled with Chinese people because there aren't that many Indian people in his neighborhood, which is predominantly Chinese and Latino.

Around two years ago, Randy started playing handball with the Chinese kids at the local park. That's how he met Shirley and picked up so much Cantonese. Now it's like Randy has immersed himself into my definition of Chinese-American culture. He goes to Chinatown, plays handball, and understands limited Cantonese.

Randy's cracked our code, but I think that's cool. Most of the time, I see him as a Chinese person with dark skin. And since the U.S. is, after all, multicultural, Randy's knowing Chinese seems very American.

Winnie was 17 when she wrote this. She later graduated high school and enrolled in college.

Angela Chen / Skyler Kane Kraemer

Wake-Up Call in Another World

By Maria Zaman

"Whoa! You must be kidding," I thought as I looked at the mud cubicle. It was a stall-like structure, just tall enough to reach my shoulders. I had no choice but to squat. Was this the bathroom? It didn't even have a faucet, toilet paper—or a toilet! Just a watering can and a hole in the dirt. My cousin told me if I had to do anything besides urinate, I'd have to go into the fields behind their house.

I was visiting relatives in Pakistan, where my dad grew up. Before arriving, I'd thought the living conditions there would be just like my home in New York. There'd be a neat row of houses, with cars lined up bumper to bumper, and kids playing hopscotch or riding their bikes. There would be sofas and fancy kitchens and bathrooms. Instead I encountered dirt roads, bed sheets for doors, and cots for beds.

I was 12, and I'd never had any real experience with poverty, other than watching advertisements for charities on TV. I felt pity, but that was it—I didn't feel attached to the people on the screen. I knew I could just flip the channel and escape them.

My four cousins, ranging in age from 13 to 22, had just one room that served as their bedroom, guestroom, and dining room. Next to that was a small kitchen. My older cousins worked as teachers in elementary schools. As I would soon learn, they were well off compared to some others in my father's village, GujarKhan.

I was shocked. Each one had their hands outstretched, begging, pleading for money.

This really hit me when my mom and I took a walk to the bazaar, the village's shopping area. Various stores were arranged next to each other by type—books, shoes, clothing—in the alleys branching out from the streets. The scent of clean air intertwined with the fragrance of sweets was exhilarating. We walked in tune to the melodious sounds coming from the alley of music stores. Shop owners called out to us, "Ajow, ajow behan-ji. Capre dekho." ("Come, come miss. Look at the clothes.")

Yet, there were many people—five or six in each alley—wearing barely any clothes. They were the beggars. What little the women wore was dirty and tattered. Men with missing arms and legs sat, calling out to us in deep, raspy voices. Their unshaven faces and dirty nails seemed to tell their story. I was shocked. Each one had their hands outstretched, begging, pleading for money. Those not sitting on the ground followed us, their hands brushing against our clothes. I felt as if I were being stalked.

They kept on hassling us for money. "Allah tumhe khush rakeh," they said. ("May God keep you happy.") I noticed my mom would look at them twice, as if to see if they truly needed it. I was upset, because I thought it was obvious they needed it. Their voices were desperate for money. Yet when she gave money to one, another would appear.

I was torn. I felt like giving all of them money. But I thought, "Hey, they must've messed up before in life, so now they're paying for it." I believed they'd somehow played a role in how they'd ended up, since I thought all adults could mend any situation.

Then I spotted about nine kids ranging from around 7 to 13 years old. They were roaming around the bazaar, trying to sell sugar cane. They were all small and skinny. Their faces were smeared with dirt and their clothes were torn and too small. Their dirty hands were ragged with cuts and calluses from the blades they used to cut the cane.

They took a break from selling to play tag. Their laughs echoed throughout the bazaar. It reminded me of when I used to play tag with my friends. We'd run swiftly to base and laugh out loud, panting for breath. When we played tag, we were in our own little world, where nothing could affect us. Were these kids ever that carefree?

Then I began to think back to the adults. What if they'd been those little kids many years ago? That would mean they'd grown up in poverty, never experienced life without it. I felt so angry, knowing that these kids already had their fate written. I felt let down by society.

Returning home to Brooklyn, it was as if I'd been tossed from a palace to the alley behind it, and back into the palace. I felt alienated as I entered my home, as if I'd never really seen it before. I looked twice at my kitchen counter, carpeting, air conditioners, and everything else.

This home I'd carelessly called my own since birth, I now cherished. I'd come to realize that I had much—maybe too much. Maybe I didn't deserve all these luxuries; maybe they were given to the wrong person. So many things in our home were only there for decoration—the paintings on the walls, the huge vases of fake flowers. I felt like I was living in a fake house, a house that was there for show and tell.

Yet I also began to see why my dad worked 14-hour days at his construction job, coming home with dirty hands and splattered jeans. The reason was us, his family. He'd grown up in Pakistan. He knew what it was like to live without luxuries.

The image of the homeless of Pakistan nagged me for a long time. I was so confused and angry. I began questioning the biggest support in my life, Allah (God). How could he do this? Why didn't he help the helpless and the innocent?

Finally I spoke to my mom about it. She told me, "Maria, Allah does what he does, but we don't always know the reason. Who knows? Maybe each and every one of those poor people will go to Janna (heaven), and Allah will shower them with his love. Maybe this is their test in life. Allah made some people rich, and some poor. We should be thankful for what we have, and not judge others by their wealth."

I knew I couldn't completely fix the problem, but I could do something.

Mom's answer gave me some comfort, for who knew? Maybe the people who had a troubled existence in this life would die to see a beautiful one in the hereafter. But I wasn't entirely satisfied. Why would Allah let them live such a life? If he loved all his people, why treat them differently?

I felt sad for the people in this never-ending system of poverty. I felt as if they were in a trap, with no escape. The full impact of this idea struck me when I saw two TV programs soon after returning from Pakistan. In one, a man went to Afghanistan and handed out money to any poor person he spotted. I thought, "OK. Now what?" A few coins might buy someone a meal today, but what will they do tomorrow? Another documentary showed me that poverty exists all over the world, not just in Pakistan. I felt overwhelmed and helpless.

I prayed to Allah for help. I made dua (prayer) for the people I'd seen, and for the millions more I hadn't. Even this didn't satisfy me entirely. I wanted to see some concrete answer to my duas. I was sure the responsibility for this situation was shared, between Allah and me. I thought to myself, "I could do so much more. Why not try to fulfill this need by doing something on my own?"

I began to recognize my drive to help the homeless and poor in the world. I knew I couldn't completely fix the problem, but I could do something. I realized I wanted to make it my career to help these people and others like them. Not just the poor, but people suffering from all kinds of injustice—political prisoners, abused women, child soldiers. I wanted to be a humanitarian.

For now, I've joined Global Kids, a human rights organization in New York City. And with the help of my friend Ayda, I've co-founded the first-ever chapter of Amnesty International in my school. Amnesty International is an organization that writes letters to government leaders pressuring them to correct human rights violations in their country. It works to help political prisoners, find missing persons, and more.

I also recently spoke to Claire Hajaj, a communications officer at UNICEF. (UNICEF is a United Nations organization working to protect the rights of children and women around the world.) I wanted to find out how young people can get involved in humanitarianism. She broke it down into three steps.

First, make change in your own community. You don't have to go far to find people who need your help. Second, fundraise for a cause. Something as small as a bake sale can have a big impact. And third, make sure your voice is always heard. Speak to those who can influence change, like government officials and religious leaders. She pointed out that youth have a particular knack for activism, since they often feel more passionate than adults about their beliefs.

I think that's true of me. I can't help it—passion and concern flow through my veins and into my very bones. Humanitarian work brings me alive. And I want to keep this drive within me always, by joining forces with others who share my dedication. I know I can't begin my career until I graduate from college. But that doesn't mean I can't start making a difference now.

Maria was 17 when she wrote this story.
She later attended Simmons College.

Joseph Vega

Unwelcome in the Hood

By George Yi

When I was about 9 years old, my father bought a candy store in Bay Ridge, a neighborhood in Brooklyn, New York. My family worked in the store and lived there too. I used to sleep in a small room in the back.

Knowing that we were about the only Chinese family in the area, I expected mistreatment from the people around there. Most of our new neighbors were Italian and I had heard rumors that Italians didn't really like Asians. I expected to live lonely and remain a prisoner inside the store.

Then, about a week after we'd moved in, I saw two Italian kids sitting on a stoop around the block. They approached me and greeted me nicely. We became good friends; in fact, they were my best friends at the time. We'd play all day long with our G.I. Joes and Superman toys and have fun. I felt no racism from these kids or their parents. They made me feel welcome. For the two years I lived there, I was content.

When I was 11, my dad told me that we were going to move again. I agreed to go with him to look at the new house one weekend, to see how I liked it. We took the train to 225th Street in the Bronx. The neighborhood, located near the Hudson River, was calm and serene. It seemed as if the only thing I could hear was the water floating by.

I saw our new house and its front yard. It looked very appealing. Inside, there were three different rooms, all large, at least much larger than the store space. I liked the place and its quiet environment. I wanted to live there. My dad let me go for a walk to explore the neighborhood. I went down to the corner grocery store and found a group of older black teenagers hanging around on the street. As I passed them, I heard one of them say, "Ch-nk."

Every time I walked through the streets, I felt my blood pressure rise.

I was infuriated. I wanted to punch one of them, but I refrained. I wasn't afraid of them; I just didn't want to throw the first punch. I continued walking but my fists were ready for action. Suddenly, a younger black boy, about 6 years old, came up to me and started talking to me in a fake Chinese accent. He muttered a lot of gibberish. That got me really mad. Why do people have to make fun of someone's language just because they don't understand it? I wanted to hit that kid so bad; I wanted to punch him till he hit the floor. But I didn't. I maintained my composure and walked past him as if nothing had happened.

I was not prepared for this. I had never been insulted that way before. When I got home, I decided not to tell my parents. I thought about it and decided it was a personal matter. I also didn't want them to worry about me. But that walk changed my perception of the neighborhood from a tranquil place to a place where racism was in your face. During the move from Brooklyn to the Bronx, I felt pain. As I carried box after box into my new home, I felt the life drain away from me.

Life in the new neighborhood was frustrating. I felt alone and left out. I was constantly confronting racism and stereotypes. It seemed like every time I passed some black teenagers, I saw expressions of hatred for me on their faces.

One time at the train station, on my way to school, I saw three towering black figures standing in my way. I said, "Excuse me." They slowly moved away but gave me a really mean look—as if I had physically hurt their parents. As I walked away, they turned around immediately and started to talk that fake Chinese gibberish. I walked up the stairs to the elevated train station and didn't turn back. They kept taunting me and trying to make me angry. When I didn't respond, they spoke louder. I just kept walking with an empty feeling in my bones.

It was upsetting that I had to live in a neighborhood that didn't accept me because of my skin color and facial features. Every time I walked through the streets, I felt my blood pressure rise. So, every chance I got, I tried to leave the Bronx to go somewhere else. Since I went to school in Manhattan, I would stay there or go to a schoolmate's house.

One day, a year after I had moved to the Bronx, I decided to do something different. It was a very nice day out and none of my school friends wanted to do anything. So, I decided to walk around the neighborhood. I was determined to ignore the racist people and have fun.

I walked down 225th Street and entered a pizza shop. The pizza smelled good and fresh, so I decided to buy a slice. Inside, I saw a bunch of black and Hispanic teenagers getting slices and playing arcade games in the back. I ate my pizza and headed for the back room to play a game. The other teenagers gave me a deep stare as I approached the machines. I saw one black kid playing Street Fighter II, one of my favorite games, so I decided to challenge him. 'Would you mind if I join in?" I asked.

He responded, "No. No problem." I inserted my quarter. The two of us ended up playing for hours, until we ran out of money.

Although we were game fighting, we were also making friends. I asked him his name, and he responded, "Andrew." After that day, we continued meeting at the pizza place, bringing more and more quarters each time. After a while, we decided to do other things together, like bike riding. We would race distances of up to 20 blocks without stopping, not even for cars. We rode around until day turned to night.

Andrew respected me. He never made fun of me or insulted my race. He even supported me at times when other people disrespected me. One time when Andrew and I were walking near my house we saw two black kids, one older than me and one younger (I think they were brothers). Andrew quickly stood in front of me as we approached them. The boys started to speak the gibberish that was supposed to sound like Chinese. Andrew said, "Shut up. Don't you got something better to do than insult a Chinese kid?" They shut up and didn't speak another word. I was glad to know that someone was my right-hand man for a change.

Sometimes it feels like a safe haven, living in a mostly Asian neighborhood.

After getting to know Andrew, I met other black and Hispanic kids around the parks and the arcade. We all got along just fine. I finally felt welcome in my neighborhood. On weekends, I would go hang out with my new friends, play at the arcades, and ride my bike through the streets. I no longer had to choose between staying trapped in my house or leaving the Bronx. I felt more free and more lively. Some teenagers around the neighborhood still made racial remarks to me, but it didn't bother me as much anymore. I knew that not everyone was against me.

After three years of living in the Bronx, my family moved again. Now, I live in Chinatown. Sometimes it feels like a safe haven, living in a mostly Asian neighborhood. I immediately felt like I belonged.

After the way I was harassed when I first moved to the Bronx, I developed a stereotype that all black people were bad and looking for trouble. I'd see some black kids walking around and think that they were looking for some Chinese kids to pick on. Day after day, I would expect to hear insults and fake Chinese accents from people who didn't know me.

It took my friendship with Andrew to show me that not all black people fit that stereotype. I've learned that you can't let a few bad experiences turn you against a whole group of people. You have to keep an open mind.

Although I haven't kept in touch with my friends in the Bronx, I have made new friends, of all races, at my school. I'm glad that I've gotten to know some black and Hispanic people firsthand instead of just hearing stereotypes about them from my Chinese friends. It gives me a better perspective on the world. I've stopped judging people based on their race; now I try to get to know them as individuals.

George was 16 when he wrote this story. He later got a degree in computer science from Columbia University.

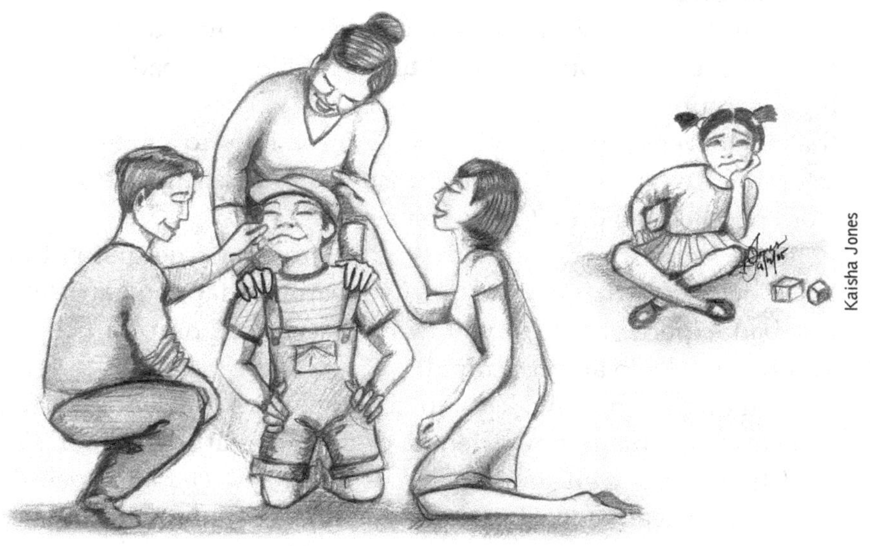

What's a Girl Worth?

By May Mai

"The baby will be a girl," said my mother. She was standing by the bathroom door as I washed my face. She was pregnant and had just gone to the clinic for a check-up.

"Oh! How do you know?" I asked.

"The doctor told me," she said sadly.

"That will be great. I want to have a sister," I said. I really didn't care what my new sibling would be, but I was trying to make my mother feel better. I knew she was anxious about having a baby girl because my grandmother wanted her to have a boy.

In China, where my family is from, sons are valued more than daughters. That's because traditionally when a daughter grows up and gets married, she goes to live with her husband's family. But a son will stay by his family's side forever, look after his parents in their old age, and take on the responsibility of the family's work after they retire.

When my mother found out she was pregnant again last February, my family was very happy about it, especially my grandmother, who'd always told my mother how much she'd love to have another grandson. So when my mother came back from the clinic with the news that it would be a girl, my grandmother was in despair. She asked my 36-year-old mother to keep having babies until she has a boy.

When my mom told my sister Judy and me about that, we were angry. How could she even say such a thing to my mother? What would happen if my mom just kept having more girls? My parents would be stuck with more mouths to feed and my grandmother would still be unhappy.

Even though my grandmother now lives in America, she's never let go of the idea that boys are more valuable than girls. She's afraid of being alone in her old age if she doesn't get another grandson. And there's some truth behind her fear. Even in America, most Chinese families I know still follow the tradition where women leave their families to go live at their husbands' houses. So to my grandmother, my sister, and I are only part of the family temporarily, while a boy would stay with her forever.

Boys have become even more valuable ever since China created the "One-Child Policy."

Boys have become even more valuable ever since China created the "One-Child Policy" in 1979. That's when the government decided that, to prevent overpopulation, women weren't allowed to have more than one child each. The policy still exists today.

When a woman is discovered to be pregnant with a second child, a representative of the Chinese government warns her to have an abortion immediately. If she doesn't, I've heard that the woman could be punished by losing her job or having to pay fines equivalent to a few years' salary for each parent. In some villages, though, I'm told that officials actually encourage women to have a second or third child so fines can be imposed. The money they collect belongs to the local government, but corrupt officials sometimes keep the money.

That happens in the Chinese village I lived in before moving here at age 11. But since most of the women in my village are poor farmers and can't afford the fines, they have to run away to hide from the officials. Fortunately, my mother could afford the fines for us while we were in China, since my grandparents and other relatives sent us money from New York. My mother paid about $1,525 for me, her second child, and about $2,000 for her third-born child, a son. She didn't mind the fine because she was able to get a boy, like my grandmother wanted.

But my little brother ended up having serious health problems. Last year, when he was 6, we found out he had a tumor in his brain that was causing his left side to be weaker than his right, making it difficult for him to walk. He had brain surgery that spring. The surgery was successful but his emotions changed afterwards. He started having uncontrollable outbursts and sometimes even yelled at my grandparents. My grandparents wanted to have a healthy grandson. That's why my grandmother asked my mom to have another kid.

My grandmother also prefers boys because she thinks they're better at earning money. When my mother and other cousins immigrated to America, they worked at cafes and found the jobs so exhausting and difficult that they quit. Now they're unemployed and the only people in our family with jobs are men.

I think that's part of the reason my grandmother treats my sister and me like we're not important. We never even met my grandmother until she came to China to see my brother when he was born, when I was 10 and my sister was 11. She came to see him, not us. She treats my sister and me well, but not as well as she treats my brother. It makes me feel uncomfortable and confused. How can she treat her grandchildren differently because of our gender?

I think my grandmother even values men more than she values herself. She was born in a poor family. She wasn't allowed to arrange her own marriage and she didn't meet my grandfather until their wedding. Her father decided everything for her and she says she appreciates all he did for her. Since then, she has believed daughters have no right to choose their own spouse.

Her ideas make me feel like I can't decide my own future. I want to go to college, major in math, and become a math teacher, but my family has asked me to be a policewoman or a nurse when I grow up. When I get married, I know I'll go live with my husband's family because that's our tradition and I feel I have to follow it. It makes me angry to feel so trapped by my culture. But at the same time, I know that if I go against the traditional female role that may mean the end of my relationship with my family, and I'm not willing to risk that.

I think my grandmother values men more than she values herself.

My mother doesn't completely share my grandmother's views. She doesn't want to have more children. She thinks it will be a burden for my father, who's the only one who works. On the other hand, she doesn't want to disappoint my grandmother. So, she has compromised with my grandmother. She'll try one more time after this baby and hope that the next child—her 5th and final one—will be a boy.

As for me, I just want my future sister to be healthy. I also don't want her to grow up with the same pressure and family structure that I've grown up with. I hope that things change, but I don't think they will. I think she'll still have to follow our own traditions even though she'll be nearly a generation younger than me. But I do think my future sister might rebel against the tradition more, since she'll be American-born. And I hope she does.

May was in high school when she wrote this story.

Cezary Ladocha

Dreams of America, Memories of China

By Chun Lar Tom

I walked slowly through Prospect Park in Brooklyn, New York. It was quiet and peaceful. Little birds flew from one branch to another. The wind hummed. A yellow leaf fell down gently in front of me. Suddenly, I realized time flies and fall was already here. "Oh, I've been here for three years," I thought. I picked up the leaf and stared at it. My memory went back to one day the same season three years ago, when I was 15 years old in China.

I grew up in a small village in southern China called Maoping, surrounded by green hills and huge flat fields. On that beautiful evening, I rode my bike home from school as the setting sun brushed reds and yellows across the western sky. The green fields had turned golden. When I got home, my mother told me that almost all of our family would be going to America in a few months.

For a moment, I couldn't think. Excitement came over me so suddenly and quickly that I felt like an expanded balloon ready to pop. I wanted to run, jump, fly, and tell the world that I was going to America. But instead, I just stood there like a fool with a big smile on my face.

I'd heard people talk about America and had long wondered about it. "They have those extremely tall and big buildings. If you get up to a top floor and put your hand out of the window, you can touch the clouds," my friend Ying told me.

"Also, people there have green eyes and red hair," she added. "They must look like those TV characters in the Japanese cartoons."

"Who told you that?" I asked suspiciously.

"My neighbor. Trust me, he knows a lot."

America seemed like a fairy world to me. I couldn't wait to go there. I imagined myself walking on a clean street with some cartoon-like people, breathing fresh morning air and passing by beautiful buildings.

"Ma, do you know what America looks like?" I asked her one day as we were preparing for the move.

"Well, I don't know," Mom answered. "I'm sure it's very rich. If not, why do so many people want to go there?" Mom was just like me. She knew nothing about America except that it's rich and powerful.

"Goodbye, my dear village," I whispered, and then stepped onto the bus, letting it drive me to my unknown future.

The day before we left, six of my friends came to my house to say goodbye. We talked about the days we'd spent together and wondered when we'd meet again in the future. Then, the room was quiet. Nobody talked. We could hear the clock murmuring in its monotonous tone that time was still going forward. And soon, we'd be separated.

"Hey, don't forget us when you get there," Ling said.

"I'll send you letters and pictures and you have to write me back, OK? You promise?" Bao said. She looked at me seriously and held my hand tightly until I said, "Yes, I will. I swear."

I looked at my friends carefully, from one to another, trying to mark their faces into my brain. I felt so sad. Suddenly, I didn't want to leave my friends and this beautiful familiar village.

We left at midnight the next day. Many of our relatives and neighbors came over to see us off. "Have a safe trip," they said with big smiles on their faces and red eyes from crying. Grandmother and Grandfather, who were staying behind, held me tightly in their arms. "Be a good girl," they said. They gave me a red envelope with money in it, wishing me good luck. I felt the fear and excitement of a new life.

We finally had to get on the bus. I took a last look at my house and my sleeping Maoping. "Goodbye, my dear village," I whispered to myself, and then stepped onto the bus, letting it drive me to my unknown future. I began to cry.

The plane trip was almost a day long. When we got to Brooklyn, New York, we moved in with my aunt, who had immigrated to America when I was a toddler. My cousin took me out to get a look at Manhattan. I was so happy that I was finally going to see the cartoon-like people and the extremely tall buildings. But I didn't see many people with red hair and green eyes. And the buildings didn't reach the clouds. It was just a myth.

I wasn't too disappointed, though, because I was drawn in by diverse new faces. I saw people with light skin, blond hair, and blue eyes. Some people wore long colorful dresses and scarves that covered their heads. Others had dark, healthy-looking skin, braided hair, and long eyelashes like a Barbie doll. Seeing these new looks made me feel like the happiest person in the world.

However, my happiness vanished over the next few days because I couldn't read English signs and maps. I got lost so easily on the subway that I couldn't go anywhere by myself. I became extremely bored and lonely because I had no friends and didn't start school for two months.

I remembered how much I liked being alone when I was in China because being alone meant being relaxed. I used to walk around Maoping by myself and climb up hills to see the sunset. I loved to lie on the grass, watching birds. I forgot time and my worries.

But I felt miserable being alone in the U.S. Being alone here meant sitting home, staring at the walls. My parents had to work late every day and my siblings had already started school.

I felt like a little tree that was uprooted and transplanted into a huge desert.

As time went by, I was eaten up by loneliness. I missed my friends. I wrote to them often. I thought about my village frequently and realized how much I'd left behind. There I had my grandparents. There I had my best friends who grew up with me. There I had a lovely home where I'd lived for 15 years. I'd loved the idea of coming here, but now I hated being here.

When I first started high school, I was lost, confused, and frustrated. I felt like a little tree that was uprooted and transplanted into a huge desert. New cultures, new people, and a new language were like a fierce sun shining on me, making me dizzy. I wanted to escape.

"Ma, can I go back home please?" I asked one day. "I don't know anything here. I don't know how to speak English. I feel so stupid."

"No," she said. "You'll never grow up if you don't try to solve your problems. Escape is not a way to overcome obstacles."

So I had to stay. But gradually, I realized my mother was right. I slowly started to adjust to this new environment. Little by little, I learned the language and culture with help from new friends at school. I no longer felt lonely. They were there for me if I didn't understand anything or needed help. I appreciated them.

Three years passed quickly and I accomplished many things. I learned how to get around the city by myself. I joined the

National Honor Society at school and had a chance to visit Washington, D.C.

Coming out of the train station into the warm sunlight during an autumn day, I walked toward Prospect Park. I wandered alone. Yellow leaves flew softly down as the breeze blew. They lay quietly on the ground with the sort of loneliness that I had when I first came here.

"Excuse me!"

A sound suddenly jumped into my head and pulled me back to reality from my memories. I looked up. A stranger was standing in front of me. "Hi. Did you see a red bag somewhere around here?"

"No, no," I said. I looked at my hand; the yellow leaf was still there. I put the leaf down and strode forward.

Chun Lar was 18 when she wrote this story.

Kenneth Ng

Thinking Twice About Race

By Luce Tang

My friends and I are a mixed group: one is black, one is white, two are Asian (including myself), and two are Hispanic. But sometimes, one of us will make a racist joke. I don't find those jokes very funny. Though I usually laugh at them, I feel uncomfortable about it. It bothers me to stereotype a whole group like that.

One reason why I feel uncomfortable is that I know what it feels like to be the "different" one. When I first moved into a black neighborhood four years ago, people's reactions to me made it clear that I was the only Asian around. A few residents actually picked on me because of my race and made me feel unwanted.

Previously, I'd lived in a fairly diverse neighborhood in Brooklyn, New York, alongside Asians, whites, Hispanics, blacks, and Hasidic Jews. Walking around, I'd see many different kinds of faces in the stores and on the streets. I like the atmosphere of indifference in a neighborhood where people are familiar with your presence and aren't alarmed.

My school, too, is packed with students of different races and nationalities who mix with each other without a problem. My friends at high school are of different races—Asian, black, white, Middle Eastern, and Hispanic, and some of them are biracial. But this ethnic diversity isn't the case in my new neighborhood. Nearly everyone in St. Albans, a neighborhood in Queens, New York, is black.

My friends' racist jokes make me uncomfortable because I know what it feels like to be the "different" one.

Soon after I moved there, when I boarded a bus to get to the subway, I got the "stink eye"—an angry glare from the corner of the eyes—from people who were standing at the bus stop. They gazed at me from head to toe. It was creepy and made me feel uncomfortable. Some guys at the corner store would holler at me, "Hey, Chun Li, come over here. I want to speak with you." I wasn't used to guys yelling at me like that and it made me self-conscious. That feeling was made worse by what they called me—a character from the video game Street Fighter.

I hear a lot of rude and discriminatory remarks walking around city streets, but I didn't expect that from people in a nice area. St. Albans is a suburban-style neighborhood with detached houses with lawns, garages, and driveways. I was also surprised that the people picking on me because of my race were black. I thought that they must know how it feels to be discriminated against, so they would try not to treat another minority as an outsider.

Not everyone treated me that way, though. I met Aeisha, who's my age, and her brother Garrett, who's a year younger than I am, while waiting for the bus. We'd often see each other because we live a block apart and take the same bus on the way to school. They'd just moved here, too.

I met Aeisha and Garrett one day when their mother was with them. "I see you some days, getting on the bus in the morning and getting off the bus in the evening," she said. "Do you live around here?"

We started talking. They made the neighborhood seem friendlier. Once I went over to their house and played chess and watched TV with them. And when I got locked out of my house when it was raining, it was comforting that I could go over to their house and wait there until someone came home to open the door.

Aeisha and Garrett, who are black, made friends with some of the other kids in the neighborhood. I gained confidence after that to make some friends of my own. Within a few months, some of my new friends took me around the neighborhood to introduce me to everybody else.

To my surprise, I met people my age who had never met an Asian person before. They said they only saw Asians on TV or in a textbook. I was shocked that they lived in New York but hadn't experienced the city's diversity. It made me feel sad, because there's so much opportunity here to learn about other cultures. I started to think that maybe this lack of experience with other groups leads to intolerance and racially-based comments and insults.

A few months later, on my bus ride home from school, a group of young teenagers sitting behind me started making comments like, "What is she doing in a black neighborhood?" and, "What is she doing with those braids?" (I wore my hair in cornrows that day.) I was angry and wanted to confront them. But I was outnumbered, and I didn't want to get into a fight. Instead, I imagined turning around and saying to them, "If you think I shouldn't wear my hair in braids because braids are strictly for black people, then why do you wear your hair straight?"

When one kid pulled my hair, though, I got furious. I turned around and told him not to touch my hair. He continued once or twice more. Then he got bored and his friends found something besides me to talk about. They got off at the stop before me. My anger lingered after they left.

I started to distrust everyone in my neighborhood. I decided not to talk to anyone there. Some of my new neighbors and friends tried to smile and call to me from across the street when I passed by. I just walked by them like I didn't hear them.

I was still feeling angry from the bus incident and felt that they were only trying to be friendly out of pity, because they felt bad that I wasn't being accepted in my neighborhood. I don't want people to be nice to me out of pity but rather because I'm pleasant to be with.

But after about a month, I realized that it was only a few people around who were ignorant and mean. Sometimes, the negative actions of a few can undo the positive actions of many. I realized I had wronged those who had been genuinely friendly. And over a period of six months, I noticed a change in the way people look at me. I no longer got that "outsider" glare. Now, for the most part, people don't really look at me at all. Once in a while, I'll get a "Good morning," or "Hi, Luce."

My experience convinced me that it's important to get to know other ethnicities besides your own.

I like that I can walk around now without feeling like a stranger in my own neighborhood. It also feels good to have established what I think is a positive reputation. Since people in my neighborhood didn't know much about Asians, I felt I had the responsibility to represent my ethnicity (Chinese-American) and my race (Asian). It was important to me that people in the neighborhood saw me as a respectable girl.

I don't regret living in St. Albans. My experience has convinced me that it's important to get to know other ethnicities besides your own. I feel that this is a necessary issue in a multilingual, multi-ethnic country like ours. Of course, I'm angry that I had to deal with racist comments when I first moved there, but I held stereotypes about African-Americans, too, like they're more likely to go into illegal businesses and more likely to get into fights over minor things. But the people in my neighborhood have normal jobs and nice homes. And now that I feel more a part of the neighborhood, I see that the people in St. Albans have a strong sense of community.

My friends and I do talk about race sometimes. If one of us makes a racist joke, another one of us will say something like, "Hey, alright, the joke is dead, let's talk about something else." Or, "You're overdoing it." We've discussed how certain jokes can be made, at least among friends, but how other jokes are downright hurtful and shouldn't be spoken at all.

In New York City, which is so mixed, there's no excuse for racism. I think we need more youth centers where people of different cultures can spend time with each other and work together on community projects. When I have kids, I'll take them to places where they can learn about different cultures. I'll teach them to have pride in their culture—or cultures—and respect other cultures as well.

Luce was 17 when she wrote this story.
She later attended college.

Holding On to Who I Am

By Zaineb Nadeem

When I was 12, my family and I moved to the United States from Faisalabad, a city in Pakistan. My parents brought me and my two brothers here so that we could go to American schools and colleges, which would help us get good jobs.

Two days after we arrived, my mother told me something I'd never heard her say in Pakistan: "Always remember who you are and never be afraid of people talking about you." My father added, "People from different countries live here and they might criticize you for your looks and language, but remember who you are and speak up if you feel you have to. Try to be a confident girl." I remember listening to them with my eyes down. I didn't know what they were talking about.

Back in Pakistan, everyone around me looked the same and believed the same things. I didn't understand how much my culture made me who I am. And I didn't understand that I would have to make sacrifices to hold on to my identity. But I started to learn as soon as I entered my first American classroom.

On my first day of school, I had a big smile on my face as I walked into my 8th grade class. I was expecting to make lots of friends, just as I had in Pakistan. I didn't think twice about my clothes.

I was wearing what I'd worn all my life, the traditional dress for females in Pakistan: a loose, long shirt that goes a little above the knee, pants and a long scarf around my neck. All of my body was covered except my head, neck, and hands. In my culture and religion (I'm Muslim), a girl is supposed to hide her body so men don't think of her as their property. You only show your body to the person you're going to marry.

As I entered the class, I noticed that there were black and white students and no Pakistani kids. Lots of the girls were wearing jeans and short tops. No one was dressed like me.

For the first week, I smiled and said hi to everybody I knew from my class. They said hi back, but coldly and with a smile that seemed unfriendly and strange. They stared at my clothes, looking at me from top to bottom. I felt so bad. I wanted to hide.

They stared at my clothes, looking at me from top to bottom. I wanted to hide.

About three weeks later, I was sitting at a cafeteria table apart from everybody. A black girl sat down, asked me my name and then, "Why do you wear this dress in school?"

"It is my cultural dress," I replied.

She told me I should change the way I dress. I didn't know much English at the time (my native language is Urdu), so I didn't ask why. But I started to think that if I changed my dress, that girl and I might become friends. I considered talking it out with my mom, but I knew my parents would be very hurt if they saw me changing to be like the other kids. My family's love was more important to me than having friends just for the time I spent in school. So I accepted feeling lonely.

Luckily, after about five weeks, I left that school because my family moved. My new middle school was an international school with Chinese, Russians, Bangladeshis, and more, including Pakistanis. I was excited to meet people from my country. I thought I would be more comfortable with them and we would understand each other.

Soon I became friends with a group of seven Pakistani girls from my class. They were good students. I wanted to be part of their group because they seemed to share my goal to get the most out of school. My new friends dressed in American clothes. There were other Pakistani girls who wore traditional clothes, but they didn't pay attention in class.

Our friendship happened easily. We started sitting together at lunch and walking together on the playground. I talked to them about movies, songs, and school, just like I'd talked to my friends back in Pakistan. But from the beginning, we were also different.

My friends talked to each other about dating, and I felt a little uncomfortable knowing that they were going against our culture's beliefs. We don't date or have sex with anyone we're not planning to marry. But since they weren't trying to include me in those conversations, I didn't let it bother me much.

Then, after a few months, one of my friends came up to me after school and started talking about the guy she went on a date with. She told me, "We are planning to have sex." This was the first time in my life anyone had talked to me about sex directly. When she started describing hugging and kissing her boyfriend, I was scared.

Sex isn't discussed in Muslim houses in front of the children, because it's believed that it will seduce them into having it. Every Muslim child knows that it's wrong to talk about sex. So when she began talking, all I wanted was for her to stop. I was afraid I would be seduced into having sex. Even if I wasn't, I was afraid talking about it might have a bad effect on my reputation, and I was afraid somehow my mom would find out that I was talking about sex.

But I didn't want to upset my friend by saying that I thought it was wrong to date and have sex. Plus, according to my culture, it's her family's duty, not a friend's, to tell her what is wrong and what is right. So instead, I tried to change the topic by talking about history class. When she kept on talking about sex, I left, saying that I needed to see my teacher for extra help.

"I will stay the way I am," I said. "Are we friends only if we dress alike?"

After that conversation, other friends began talking to me more openly about sex. I tried to avoid the subject. I felt more and more uncomfortable with them. I didn't want other Pakistani students, my teachers who were from my country, or my parents, to think that I was like them. I started to wish I had friends who didn't date and were more like me.

Then one day, during lunch, after we'd been friends for almost the whole school year, one of my friends started telling me that now that I am in America, I should change the way I dress and speak.

"You look like an old-fashioned girl in this dress and speaking Urdu and I think you should start dressing the way we dress." I still remember how her voice sounded, mean and nasty. My other friends agreed with her. I was angry because my clothes and language are part of me, so when they told me to change them, I felt they were trying to change my inner self.

Suddenly, I didn't feel like eating anything. A storm was building inside me. I heard my mother's voice in my head, saying, "Be confident. Say what you want to say."

"I will stay the way I am," I said. "Are we friends only if we dress alike? I love my culture, and I won't change at any cost."

They just made fun, saying, "You talk like an old woman." I hated them for saying this to me. I felt really low and lonely because they were more interested in my dress and language than in me.

I wasn't going to be friends with people who weren't going to accept me. For the first time since I'd come to the U.S., I had declared my pride in my culture. I felt more sure of who I was than ever before. But I felt like an alien, and lonely.

A week after I left my friends, I was sitting alone when a Pakistani girl in traditional dress came up to me and asked if I needed help with anything. The next day, she said hi, and from then on we started sitting together at lunch. We talked about schoolwork and I found that she was a good student. I started going to her house, something I hadn't done with my other friends. She asked me why I left my other friends and I told her the story. She agreed with what I'd done. She, too, is determined to follow our cultural traditions. We became best friends.

I'm now 17, and my best friend and I go to an international high school. These days I have friends from other cultures. We have fun together doing after-school activities like yearbook committee and student government. I enjoy talking to them about our classes, music, movies, and books.

Sometimes we talk about our cultures' traditional foods and dress, and sometimes we discuss our cultures' beliefs about sex and dating. I'm more comfortable talking about sex now because we've studied it in school. I still don't want to date before I get married or know the details of other people's personal relationships. I like knowing that when I'm married, I'll belong only to one person who will also belong only to me, and that only the two of us will know about our intimacy.

I respect the way my friends from other cultures choose to live their lives—I don't want to change them and they aren't trying to change me. The conversations we have are respectful and comfortable, and nobody tries to make fun of someone else's values and call them old-fashioned, the way my old group of friends did with me.

But I've learned I'm still not comfortable being close to a

person who doesn't share my most basic cultural and religious beliefs. My family understands me, my pride in my identity, and the choices I've made to hold on to that identity, and I want my closest friends to understand me the way they do.

Zaineb was 17 when she wrote this story.

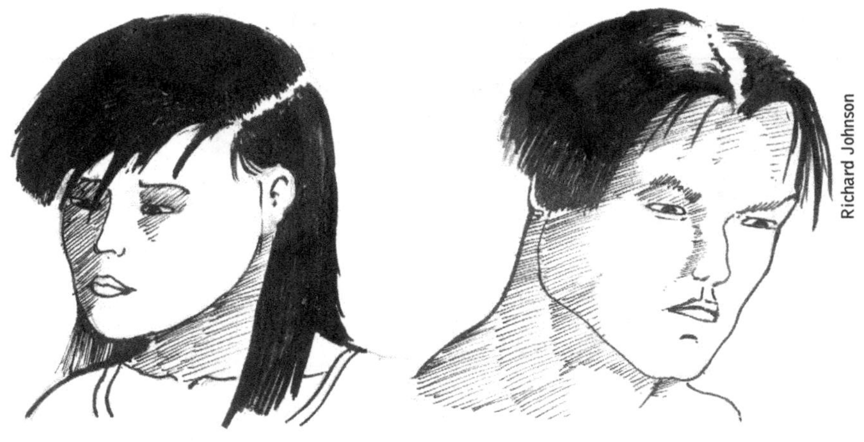

My Korean Boyfriend

By Sue Chong

My boyfriend Kevin and I went out for a year and, during that time, we fought until we got sick of it. We fought about the stupid things all couples fight about, but the main thing that came between us was something that other couples probably don't have to deal with. We constantly argued about whether I was too Americanized.

Kevin and I both came to the U.S from Korea five years ago. Although we had this in common, we had different points of view on everything. He would ask me why I couldn't be like other Korean girls. If I were a "real" Korean girl, I would listen to him when he told me to do something, depend on him for most things, and think his way instead of my way. When I didn't agree with him, we would have another fight. To me, he was too

Korean and too narrow minded. He refused to accept any culture except his own, and he always thought his way was the only way.

I eat Korean food, I speak Korean, I have respect for my parents as Koreans have, I celebrate Korean holidays and traditional days. I even joined the Korean Club in school, so that I can keep my customs with my friends.

But since I came to this country, I have come to love certain customs from other cultures. For example, I see the way my Hispanic friends greet people with affection. They kiss and hug when they say "hello," and I love this. (In Korea, people are much more formal; they just shake hands and bow to each other out of respect.) So I started kissing my friends on the cheek too.

Kevin didn't like this, and he told me so. He even asked me to stop it. I didn't want to, so I did it anyway but not as much. Later on, he told me not to kiss and hug other people. I asked him why, and he told me that he didn't like it and that other Koreans didn't act the way I did. He couldn't accept it.

Korean men like to tell their wives and girlfriends what to do. Kevin would always tell me how to dress and how to act in front of others. He wanted me to stay next to him all the time. I would complain that I was not his little toy and that he couldn't just order me around.

He said if I were a "real" Korean girl, I would listen to him when he told me to do something.

When I would go against his wishes, Kevin would say, "Why are you so Americanized?" I didn't know how to respond to that. He said I must be ashamed of my country and my culture to act the way I did. I was shocked, and it hurt me badly. I was not ashamed of my country or culture. I am proud of being a Korean. I just want to accept other cultures, too.

I can't deny that I sometimes act like an American, trying to be more independent and outgoing than other Korean girls. But

I still act like a Korean, too. I want to go with the flow, and that doesn't mean that I don't like my own culture. I am trying to balance two cultures. Through my boyfriend, I got a chance to think about who I really am. I realized that I am a Korean and an American, too.

Sue was 17 when she wrote this story.

Qing Zhuang

The Stranger in My House

By May Mai

Sometimes, I feel my father is a close family member. Sometimes, I feel he's a stranger. It's hard for me to judge the role he plays in my life after we spent six years separated by an ocean.

My father emigrated from China to New York City when I was 6. After he left China, my family broke apart the way a drinking glass breaks into pieces when it falls on the ground. It can be put back together, but it will never really be whole again.

Before my father went to America, we spent a lot of time together. We went everywhere together and our favorite place was an amusement park called Palace for Youth, in Tai Chang, China. There were always a lot of parents holding hands with their kids and enjoying rides, like merry-go-rounds and bumper cars or, as the Chinese call them, "peng peng che."

I spent the happiest moments of my childhood in Palace for

Youth with my family. Once when I was 5, my father, sister, and I sat on the small airplane ride and my father was scared because my sister and I pressed the buttons to make the plane go up and down every two seconds. He said to us, "Jane and May, release your hands! It's too dangerous to fly that high up. Let it down!"

My mother stood below and watched us, laughing at my father. He closed his eyes and whispered, "Please, stop flying!" It was so fun I wanted time to stop so I could remain in that moment. I loved seeing my family laugh and I felt so close to them then, especially my father.

My father was also there for me during the not-so-fun times. When I was about 6, I went to the hospital almost every week. I often got colds and fevers and I can't remember how many shots I got. But I didn't cry out when the doctors gave me shots because my father was always right next to me.

I held my father's hands tightly, as if he would fly away if I let go.

He comforted me and said, "May, you are a brave girl, like a boy. If you cry, you won't be pretty when you grow up. So don't cry, be a good girl and I will buy a lot of things for you." He worried about me and tried his best to make me happy when I was sick. He even bought a small bicycle to comfort me.

But when I learned how to ride that bicycle, my father wasn't there with me. He had left for New York the day after he bought it. He told me he was going to America to earn lots of money, so my mother, siblings, and I could go to America one day and have a better life.

I didn't know where America was. Was it far away from my hometown, Guangdong, China? When would I see him again, tomorrow or never? I held my father's hands tightly, as if he would fly away if I let go. But finally, our hands were separated and he was gone.

That first year, I felt hopeless. I didn't know where America was or whether my father would return home. As time went on, I tried to get rid of the image of him in my head so I wouldn't feel so sad, but I couldn't. We talked on the phone and wrote letters to each other, and he came back to visit at least once a year, making it impossible to forget him.

We had fun being together again whenever he visited. We'd go to a park where we'd barbecue and play around in the river. We'd splash each other until we looked like wet chickens and I'd feel happy and comfortable with my family again. As the years went by, though, my father started to become a distant relative I saw once or twice a year. We always had fun when he came, but by the time his next visit rolled around almost a year later, I'd have almost forgotten what he looked like.

When I was still little, I often asked my mom, "Who's the guy sitting in the living room surrounded by my relatives?" whenever he first arrived for a visit. My mother would stare at me and answer angrily, "That's your father." I wouldn't believe her at first. He became thinner, older, and more unrecognizable every time I saw him. When he first left for America, he only had a few gray hairs. But soon, they were uncountable. Each time when he left again, I locked myself in my bedroom. I couldn't say goodbye to him. Goodbye separated my family and I wanted us all to live together.

So when I was 11, I was happy and surprised when I heard the good news from my father: "We're all going to America." I had been waiting for this day for a long time. I imagined my family was back together, sitting in the living room as we talked, played, laughed, and watched TV together. My father had told me there were a lot of parks near our apartment in New York and I pictured my whole family there playing "owls catch chickens," a popular game in China.

The first week we arrived in New York City was the best. My father had opened a factory with three of his friends several years before, but he didn't go to work that first week we were there. His friends understood my father needed time to be with his family since we'd just moved to America.

Everything was new to us. My father showed us around Chinatown (our new neighborhood) and lower Manhattan. Then we went to the park. When we saw the swings, my sister and I ran over quickly while my parents and my younger brother walked behind us, slow as turtles. My sister and I swung up and down, forward and backward by ourselves. But I had to push hard on my parents' backs so they could swing up to the sky, too.

I pushed my father right, left, forward, and backward. He kept turning around instead of swinging up and down and his hair changed shape in the breeze. We laughed at him and he didn't mind.

But after a week, my happy life suddenly became gloomy. My father had to go back to work. It became just like the life I'd had in China when my father was gone. He worked six days a week and during what little time he spent at home, he was usually too tired to talk to us. And when he did talk to us, sometimes he got angry and yelled or even hit us for coming home late or not working hard enough. I think he was stressed from working so hard and living with all of us in a small apartment. He had never yelled or hit us in China. I was shocked and scared by his change.

I thought I'd have more time with my father once we were living together again in New York. But instead, I didn't feel my father existed, though he was sitting next to me, eating dinner, and living in the same apartment with me. I felt neglected, alone, and sad. I even thought about running away because I wanted attention from my father other than yelling and hitting. My father had changed from the fun and loving person I'd known in China to a tired, strict, distant, and angry man.

Now, six years later, it's still the same. His anger hurts me but what hurts even more is that we don't share our feelings anymore. He doesn't know when I get sick or sad. The only time we talk is during dinner when we sit together and eat. Then I have to go back to my room to study while my father goes to his room to rest. On Sundays, the only day my father doesn't work, he goes out and gambles with his friends instead of spending time with my siblings and me.

Sometimes I think he ignores me not only because he's so busy and tired. Maybe he feels I am not a child anymore, but a 16-year-old who is smart enough to do things on my own.

When he does talk to me during dinner, it's always about how he needs me to fill out a government form in English, or we fight about how late I've been out or about school. He says, "You have to study hard, go to a good university, and get a high-salary job."

I understand I have to work to achieve my father's dream for me, but it's hard for me to learn under such pressure. Plus, I do study hard, and get the highest grades in the class. But he doesn't even ask me for my grades, so he never knows how well I do. It makes me feel like he doesn't really care. I tell my mother, who I'm still close to, that I dislike school because my father pressures me so much. I feel depressed and exhausted. My mother has asked him to stop pressuring me, but he doesn't listen.

He had never yelled or hit us in China. I was shocked and scared by his change.

If I felt brave enough to speak up to my father, I'd tell him that hiding my feelings for five years is enough. I'd tell him that he's a good father, but also a bad father. He takes care of my family and gives us money for food and clothing. But I'd tell him that's not what my sister and I want. We want his time and his love. We don't want to be left out, to stay home alone while he's busy with his job. And we don't want to be yelled at.

I try to have a life of my own. I've spent a summer studying at Yale University, traveled to Turkey, and grown more independent from my family. I've made some close friends who comfort and support me. But I still miss my father. Strangely enough, we seem to get closer when we're apart. When I'm away, I think my father starts missing me and gets concerned about me.

Last summer when I was at Yale, my father called me once or twice a week to ask how everything was going. He asked about the campus, the food, my bedroom, my roommate, and curfews. Even though I figured he was asking me all this so he'd feel in control of me like he is at home, I still liked it because it made me feel he cared about me.

It's also easier for me to talk to him when I'm away. I don't feel nervous the way I do at home because on the phone he asks about my health and safety, which makes me happy. And if he does get angry, I can just hold the phone away from my ear.

Right now, I'm not ready to talk to him about my feelings—I think he'd just say I'm crazy and immature. When I grow up and move out permanently, I hope I'll be able to have a closer relationship with my father. But for now, I'm looking forward to his phone calls when I go to another summer program away from home. It may not be perfect solution, but at least we'll be having a conversation.

May was in high school when she wrote this story.

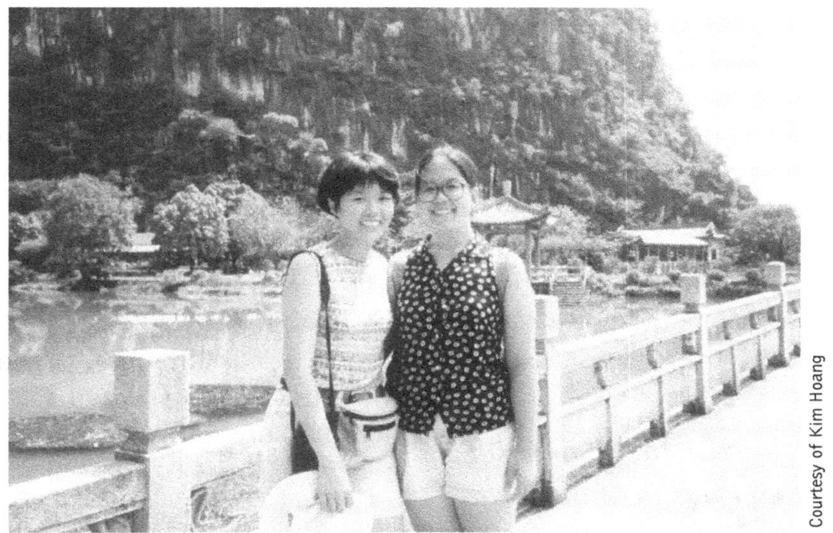
Courtesy of Kim Hoang

Kim (right) with her sister in Canton, China

Chinese in America, American in China

By Kim Hoang

When I was growing up and people asked me, "What are you?" I would immediately say that I was Chinese. I was acknowledging my Chinese roots, even though I was born and raised in New York City. But sometimes I felt stupid for not knowing more about my ancestry and about a culture that had, in fact, influenced the way I live and think.

I am American, but there are things about my life that are distinctly Chinese. I eat Chinese food every night with chopsticks. I can understand Cantonese Chinese although I can't really speak it. I go to family weddings in which the bride usually wears a white wedding gown in the morning and a cheong sam, a traditional Chinese silk dress, at the evening banquet. I celebrate the annual Chinese New Year festival with friends and family, and watch the sidewalk dragon dances in Chinatown.

These things are part of my life that came from China, a place I knew very little about. I needed to find out how much of me was Chinese and how much was American. I hoped a trip to China would bring me closer to my Chinese side, and teach me how to put it into my life.

When I mentioned an interest in traveling to China, my mom agreed immediately. My mom never forced me to learn Chinese traditions but she was pleased that I was ready to learn more about where my ancestors came from. Besides, my older sister was already there studying and I could stay with her and our relatives.

In America, I am Chinese but when I was in China, I was American.

As I left for China last summer, I hardly felt the emotions I thought I would. I didn't cry when I said goodbye to my mother. I didn't cry when the plane took off, and I didn't even cry when I began to feel ill on the plane because of all the junky airline food.

But I did cry when we landed. I remember having this great feeling of awe and excitement, and I couldn't contain it. I envisioned all the new things I was going to see and all the relatives I would finally meet. Landing was so final. There was no going back, and all I could do was soak up every ounce of culture I possibly could.

My sister picked me up at the airport in Beijing, the capital, and we boarded a minivan, China's cheaper version of a regular taxi. When we arrived at our relatives' apartment complex, I saw an 80-year-old man and woman I vaguely remembered from photographs. They were my aunt and uncle on my father's side. It turned out that the last time they had seen me was when I was 3 and they were in America for a visit.

They went on and on about how I looked so much like my father. They said this all in Chinese and I could understand every word of it. But I couldn't express my feelings. All I could do was nod and smile, and they laughed, knowing that I couldn't talk to them.

It was apparent from the first day I spent in Beijing that I had virtually no chance of sneaking into the crowd and living like a native. The fact that I couldn't understand Mandarin Chinese, the national dialect, blew my cover. (Although China has one written language, it has dozens of spoken languages. My mother taught us Cantonese, which sounds nothing like Mandarin.)

Everyone in Beijing spoke so fast and my sister, who was studying Mandarin, had to translate everything for me. Not being able to speak the language meant I had no freedom. I couldn't buy my own clothes or order my own meal. I couldn't even buy my own water. I felt like a 3-year-old who had to ask her mother for everything.

The funny thing is that when I'm in America, Chinese people on the street ask me for directions in Chinese and expect me to answer them flawlessly in the same dialect. I feel bad when I can't answer them. In China, however, people saw me and assumed that since I wore blue jeans and Nikes and carried myself differently (staring at every building with amazement and looking at every passing bicycle and every person with genuine interest, like most tourists do), I couldn't possibly understand a word of Chinese or anything about China.

People were surprised that I could understand the simplest Mandarin phrases (like, "It's time for dinner" and "Did you have fun today?") without their having to translate for me. It's like I was living in two worlds and even though I was a part of both, I didn't fit into either of them perfectly. In America, I am Chinese but when I was in China, I was American.

What made matters worse was that my sister sometimes encouraged me to be silent so that we would get better rates for things. When we bought tickets to get into the Forbidden City (the ancient home of the emperors), for example, my sister told me not to say a word. She said that many museums and parks charge a higher admission price (sometimes three times higher than for a native) if they know you're a tourist. I never found out if this was legal, but it was widely done.

Being silent made me feel all the more foreign in China. It was a constant reminder that I could never fully assimilate into life there. I stuck out, and I began to feel extremely paranoid walking down the street. I felt like I had a big sign on my back that said, "Kick me, I'm an American."

Other times, though, I felt so connected to China. One night I looked out the window next to my bed. I saw the black sky and the bright stars and I felt like I was home. Sometimes I felt like I had been there before. I saw busy street markets with people haggling for the lowest prices. Traffic was horrible, and of course, almost every face you saw was Chinese. I had seen all of this in Chinatowns in New York, Boston, and Toronto. I was surprised at the similarities, but there were differences too: in America, I can always walk a few blocks or take the subway and once again mix with people of different races and cultures.

I visited many places while I was in China, but it was Tiananmen Square that had the biggest impact on me. This was where people gathered to listen to Mao Zedong as he spoke on a rostrum high above the square. (He was the founder of Communist China.) It was also the site of the 1989 Tiananmen Square Massacre, in which thousands of students demonstrating for democracy were killed after government troops opened fire. The square is an open space where both tourists and natives hang out. Walking across the stone tiles, I remembered the news footage of Tiananmen Square, filled with tanks and chaos. I realized I was standing where many people had died for their cause, people who weren't that much older than I was.

One of the final things I did during my trip was talk to my uncle. Although I had been eager to chat with him, there never seemed to be enough time. I was always sightseeing and he worked at a chemical company during the day. I knew my uncle spoke fluent English, so talking wouldn't be a problem.

We talked for more than two hours, mostly about Tiananmen Square. My uncle said he thought that the students could have used a less dangerous method to obtain their goal and that they could have tried harder to work with the government. Although he still supports communism, he thinks that all governments have their flaws and that there will be more demonstrations for freedom in China.

I wish I could've talked with my uncle longer. He has seen so many things in his lifetime—the end of the emperors, the birth of communism—and I didn't have time to hear all that he had to say. But I was glad for what I did learn. Hearing his first-hand accounts made the recent events of Chinese history seem real to me. They weren't just facts in a book or images on a television screen anymore.

Hearing my uncle's first-hand accounts made the recent events of Chinese history seem real to me.

It's been a year since my trip to China, and the things I remember most are not the big places but the small things. The hot buses that my sister and I took to Tiananmen Square. The imitation Good Humor ice cream we bought to cool down since many of the museums didn't have air conditioning. I still want to know more about China and Chinese culture. It may be a while before I have a chance to go back, but in the meantime I'm taking Mandarin classes and I'm volunteering at the Chinatown History Museum to learn more about the Chinese in America.

I had wanted China to bring me closer to the Chinese culture and heritage I knew so little about. But the trip brought into perspective the two sides of my life. I can enjoy the freedoms I have in America, like the freedom of speech. And I can also relate to the history of China and its customs. I now realize that who I am is a combination of the two.

Kim was 15 when she wrote this story. She later graduated from Wellesley College and now works in advertising and design.

Other Ways To Be Rich

By Leneli Liggayu

I felt excited but weird as I sat down to email my cousin Michelle in the Philippines last June. A pang of guilt struck me as I typed. I'd had so many chances to keep in touch and yet I'd let seven years go by.

"Will she write back?" I wondered. "Will she like the gifts I sent?" I finished the last line, took a deep breath, and with a shaky hand pressed "Send."

I hadn't seen Michelle or my other relatives since I visited the Philippines when I was 10. I remember the moment my parents, brother, and I first stepped out of the revolving airport doors into the muggy city air of Manila, the capital of the Philippines.

It was crowded, the heat didn't feel clean, and the humidity made my throat tighten. But family was the number one reason for my nervousness. I didn't know my relatives, and I worried they might not accept their comparatively rich American relative.

My parents, who had immigrated to the U.S. before I was born, were constantly sending medicine and clothes to my aunts and uncles in the Philippines. I always assumed they were poor and didn't have any major income besides what my parents sent. I didn't understand how they could depend on my parents so much. Why were they so poor when my parents were working so hard and living a pretty good life in the U.S.?

We left the airport and took an old van to Fort Bonifacio, an hour outside Manila. Looking out the window as we drove through a few small towns, it was almost as I'd imagined it, except there were so many cars it was almost impossible to see the road below us. I also saw motorbikes pulling carriages, just a step above a horse and buggy. And the roofs of the one-room houses we passed were just wide steel panels.

When we got to the house, I sighed with relief because it was bigger than the ones we'd passed. The first floor was built deep into the ground, with a sewer system around it like a moat. The second floor towered up high past a mango tree. At least 15 relatives came out to greet us. They were friendly and that calmed my nerves.

But when I finally fell asleep that night, I was awakened by a lizard crawling into my bed. It was green and scaly and about the size of my forearm. Its eyes stared at me with interest. My scream woke the rest of my family, and I could hear giggling in the other room. I was embarrassed because I didn't want to seem weak, but I couldn't understand how someone could sleep at night with creatures roaming all over their bed.

But soon I relaxed, and I began to get to know my cousins for the first time. I had five girl cousins and two boy cousins ranging from age 2 to 17-year-old Michelle. They were all affectionate and accepting. They told me stories of their daily lives that could fill books.

My 11-year-old cousins Mari and Alea told me about the time they were behind the house taking care of the baby pigs, and one slipped from their grip. He ran for the streets, fairly quickly for something with little pig legs. They chased him, but he kept getting away. I had to giggle at the image of the little pig slipping from their hands like butter.

As more and more stories flowed from their mouths, I realized they had a pretty happy life without a lot of material things. I never heard them complain about how little they had. Instead of feeling bad for them like I once had, I felt envious of all their stories and fun. Little did I know, I would soon be part of a story that I'd get to tell.

One evening, I was sitting on the couch, playing Scrabble with my uncle and two other cousins, when a voice disturbed my train of thought.

"Let me go get ready," said my grandfather Tatay (which means father in Tagalog, the main language of the Philippines). As he walked away quietly, the only sounds I heard were my aunts picking up toys off the floor, as if someone important was coming.

I wasn't sure why everyone began to groan and moan. All I knew was that the floor was abnormally clean and everyone was sitting on a chair or the couch as if waiting for something. Then the sound of thunder breaking the night sky startled me. Rain pounded on the steel roof and began seeping under the door into the house.

"Come on! Let's go help Tatay!" my cousin Mari exclaimed. I didn't know what she was talking about but I ran off with her to my grandfather's convenience store, which was connected to the house.

She handed me a candle, some foil, and a cardboard box. "Here, follow what I do," she said. She drew a circle on the cardboard and cut it out with a razor. Then she cut a small hole inside the circle and pushed a candle through it. She wrapped a long piece of foil under the candle until it covered the cardboard circle. I finally understood: It was a candleholder.

"That's so cool!" I shouted. Tatay told me to hush. I looked over to where he was standing and saw a long line of people. Then I realized they were trying to buy what I was trying to make.

It turned out that every time a storm came around and the town lost electricity, people would run through the flooding streets to my grandfather's store to buy the candles that my grandfather and cousins would make for them.

It was hard work at first, but soon the process began to flow from my fingers and we became a two-person assembly line. I cut, I slid, I wrapped and handed off. The finished product made me feel proud. Mari and I laughed the whole time, playing with the fire on our desk in the stormy night, while our grandfather sold our works of art to his customers. When they had all gone, I made one for myself, lit it, and slid off my chair.

"Oh my gosh!" I screamed. Mari and Tatay laughed at me. The water had risen past my ankles, and I didn't understand why they weren't running to protect the house. Then it clicked. Everyone had been sitting on the chairs and couches waiting for the water to rise, and it had. It almost reached my knees now. I waded over to the living room, with the creatures of the earth—roaches, lizards, and the pet dog—swimming alongside me.

I never heard them complain about how little they had. Instead of feeling bad for them like I once had, I felt envious.

My family was sitting on desks, chairs, and couches, chatting about politics and annoying neighbors. It felt strange how everyone was having a normal conversation while the house flooded. But I found beauty in it. In that living room was the calm of the storm.

I waded over to my youngest cousins who were playing with their Barbie dolls, and I combed their hair with my fingers. Every now and then the thunder would crackle and my 2-year-old cousin would jump into my arms. After a while, my cousins led me up the stairs and we all looked out the window. Before my eyes was the most breathtaking scene I'd ever witnessed.

My view overlooked the whole town. In all the windows, I could see the candleholders I'd made. The lightning in the background lit the black sky. Rain blew onto my face and I didn't care. I saw the floodwater flowing downstream, and part of me wanted to jump in and let it take me anywhere it wanted to go. Then, almost as quickly as it began, the storm quieted. As the lights went on, I saw every one of my candles being blown out, one by one.

I'd always judged my relatives and thought of them as poor, and even pitied them. But in that moment, I realized there were other ways to be rich—in family and in happiness.

Sitting up there on the windowsill—watching the flooded streets, knowing families were spending time together in their flooded homes—grounded me. It made me appreciate the precious time with my relatives, like they appreciated life itself. Suddenly, I desperately missed all the years I hadn't experienced with my cousins.

I realized there were other ways to be rich—in family and in happiness.

A week later, I was in my room packing, and my heart was breaking. I knew it'd be years before I'd see my relatives again because it's so expensive to travel to the Philippines. I'd miss their food, laughter, and love. My mom, dad, and brother loved me without a doubt, but this love was different. This was a community of love. Their love made their lack of material things seem less important.

I rolled my suitcase down the stairs. Everyone was waiting there for me. All my aunts, uncles, and cousins kissed me and put their blessings on me. Finally, Tatay pulled me into a great big hug and gave me a kiss on my forehead. "Ingat. Mahal kita," he said. Take care. I love you.

I hugged him fiercely and kissed him goodbye. Then I ran out to the van and shut the door. I wasn't ashamed when my tears began falling.

Back in New York, I was more thankful for life and family. I became more focused on friendships and relationships. But while my parents spoke to my relatives on the phone every couple of weeks, I didn't keep in touch. My inability to speak Tagalog and their awkwardness with English made me feel shy about speaking to them.

As the months turned into years, I got caught up in my own affairs and my memories of the Philippines began to gather dust. Although I didn't completely forget about my relatives, they became distant to me. Life went on and I forgot about those emotions I'd had way back when.

But since both my grandfathers passed away recently, I've started thinking about my family again. I finally decided to set aside my guilt and get in contact with them. I bought all seven of my cousins tote bags, multi-colored rhinestone bracelets, and Old Navy T-shirts. Then I emailed my cousin Michelle, who's now 23, married, and has a baby boy, to tell her the gifts were on the way.

With these gifts, I wanted to repay my cousins for the intangible gift they'd given me. They gave me what I lacked—a community of love. I wanted to give them what they lacked—these material items—even if they didn't need them. After I emailed Michelle, I spent two weeks worrying about why she hadn't replied. Then one day I logged on and there was her response, waiting to be opened.

For a moment, I was afraid to read it. I worried it might be an angry message about how I hadn't kept in touch and how I assumed I could jump in and out of their lives whenever I pleased. I worried the connection might be gone. Then, in a rush of courage, I finally clicked "Open."

Michelle greeted me with a "Hello" and a "Thank you," saying I was kind to think of them. I was relieved when she explained that she wasn't very good with computers and that's why she hadn't replied right away.

But what made me smile from ear to ear and reassured me that my community of love was still out there waiting for me, was the line right at the end: "We love you and miss you. Hear from you soon."

Leneli was 16 when she wrote this story. She completed high school and went to college, majoring in journalism.

Money Can't Buy Love

By Lily Mai

I used to think my parents didn't love me because they seemed to value money more than they valued me. When I was young, my parents worked up to 14 hours a day, so my grandparents raised me until I was 7. They worked so hard because we were poor.

The Chinatown apartment I shared with my parents, brother, and grandparents was extremely small, with just two rooms and a kitchen. The bathtub was in the kitchen and the bathroom was in the hallway outside the apartment. My grandpa taught me to kill the roaches that were everywhere by pouring hot water on them. The refrigerator was never cold enough, the stove was covered with grease, and the kitchen wall was so spattered with cooking oil that my parents had taped calendar paper over it. My grandparents slept in one bedroom, which doubled as the living room, and my parents, brother, and I slept in the other.

At the time, it didn't bother me that we had so little, or that my parents were always at work. (My father was a chef in a Chinese restaurant and my mother made clothes in a factory.) My grandparents gave me everything to keep me satisfied. They took my brother and me to the park, school, and McDonald's. They bought us picture books and crayons, washed our hair, and even potty-trained us.

But when I was 7, my parents had saved enough money to move. My parents, brother, and I left my grandparents' apartment in Chinatown and moved to a big three-bedroom house in Brooklyn. It was nice at first because my parents were able to buy a new stove, TV, and furniture. But without my grandparents around, I began to notice the long hours my parents worked to pay rent and to buy the furniture. They had only one day off a week, and they usually spent it paying bills or shopping for things they needed. They didn't talk to or play with my brother and me.

It seemed like money was the only form of communication in our house.

When my mom was around, her role seemed to be to keep me out of trouble and make sure I did my homework. My relationship with my father was no better. He just gave us money and bought us food. It seemed like money was the only form of communication in our house.

I tried to come up with things to do on my own. I played with my Barbies, watched TV, and built tents in the living room. But I would've given up the big house and TV and gone back to live in Chinatown if I could have had my parents around. I was lonely. My parents had given me money, clothes, and food. But these were poor substitutes for love and attention.

Last summer, when I was 16, I finally realized just why they were so focused on money. We took a trip to China and went to visit their childhood homes. That's when my feelings about them began to change.

I'd always known my parents had had rough childhoods.

They'd told me things like, "If there was food on the table, then it was a good day." But I couldn't imagine their childhood until I actually saw where they grew up.

When we got to the farm where my mom grew up, in a small town near the city of Guangzhou in southeastern China, I saw that the ground was nothing but dry soil. It was like a desert with leaves, trees, and roads of endlessness ahead. There were old gray brick houses and roosters making cock-a-do-da-do noises from wooden cages. The heat was unbearable and made me itch. I kept swatting flies off my skin, and everywhere there was the sound of insects. I wanted to get away fast. I wished I'd never come.

Then I entered my mom's old house. It had two bedrooms, a kitchen in the living room, and a second floor dedicated to praying. The beds were made of flat wooden planks. There were no couches, just a row of chairs. My mom said they'd leave the door open every day because they lived in a deserted area, and dogs and roosters would come in and walk around the living room.

The stove was a box of gray bricks and there were logs under two huge holes where they'd build a fire and put a pot over it to cook. There were no machines to make things like ladders, pots or chairs, so they made them by hand instead. They had to kill animals and grow vegetables to eat. It was like living in the 17th century. I was amazed. I thought, "This is what poverty looks like."

My mom told me how in the mornings she'd go to school and learn how to read and write Chinese characters. When she got home, she'd scrub the kitchen walls or help her mother make dinner, peeling off chicken feathers and putting her hand inside the chicken to remove the insides. Or she'd wash her clothes on the porch, leaning over a bucket of water and a bar of soap on the floor. Afterward she'd make a fire and cook for my grandmother. There was no TV, CD player, or computer, so her days were spent doing things to get by. That was my mother's childhood.

It was worse than I'd expected. I wanted to look away because I felt guilty about my childhood compared to my mother's. I hoped my mother was too busy catching up with her relatives and friends to see my reaction. We visited my dad's house nearby too, and it was even smaller than my mother's.

I thought about my own home. I had my own room with my own TV, computer, and a comfy bed. I had lots of clothes to wear. I had an education. Suddenly I realized why they'd risked everything and left their relatives behind to come to a new country where they didn't speak the language, and get jobs working 14 hours a day. They did it to give me all the things they never had. Maybe they did love and care about me after all.

There have been times when I've dreamed of one day getting away from my parents and living independently. I've imagined not inviting them to my wedding or sending them money when I grow up, thinking that then they'd realize how much they hurt me. I wanted to use money against them since it seemed to be more important to them than love. But now I see that the money they worked hard for six days a week wasn't for them, but for me. I'm grateful for the long hours they worked and the money they saved to give me a better life. I hope I can pay them back when I get a job. I hope one day I can buy them something big like a car or a new house.

I see that the money they worked hard for six days a week wasn't for them, but for me.

Still, I think in trying so hard to save me from the life she had as a child, my mom overlooked something. She told me how hard she worked growing up. But she also said how she worked alongside her mother and had long conversations with her. I think that's how they developed the bond they have now.

Today, my mother talks to her mother about almost everything. They joke with each other and talk for hours about work, friends, and movies. My father has a good relationship with his parents, too. They read the newspaper together and talk about the news.

I hardly talk to my parents at all, and I can't imagine laughing with them the way my mom does with her mom. Sometimes I wish I could trade in some of the things she gave me as a child for a few hours of the closeness she and her own mother had. I don't think my mother realizes how important love and affection is to me. I think she and my dad thought that by working and buying me things, they were showing their love for me.

My parents grew up in poverty, and they worked hard so I wouldn't experience the same thing. They did a good job—I grew up in comfort and didn't struggle to survive. I had so many things. The only thing missing was my parents.

Lily was 16 when she wrote this story.
She attended Brooklyn College

A Short Cut to Independence

By Anita Chikkatur

For years, I needed my mom's help to twist my long, thick hair, which fell nearly halfway down my back, into a braid or even a ponytail. I hated that morning ritual because it made me feel helpless. I hated the long hours it took to wash and dry my hair. I wanted to feel free and independent. I wanted a haircut.

But I couldn't make myself do it. A haircut was a big decision. My hair was more than just a bunch of dead cells. It was a symbol of control.

I held back for about a year because I was afraid of what my parents would say. The last time I had it cut was when I was 10 and first came to America. For my parents and relatives, long hair is considered an essential part of being a woman. Especially for "good Indian girls." Most of my female relatives have long hair and change is not welcome. Recently when an aunt got a bob (hair cut up to the neck), my mom said, "She doesn't look good at all."

Most of my friends didn't want me to go short, either. I'm not sure why. Maybe they were like me, afraid of change. Somewhere inside, I believed that the really beautiful women had long hair. I remembered someone saying that college guys liked women with long hair. (And college is the place where you meet your husband.)

But my friend Hee Won assured me that it didn't matter what people would say. She and I used to gawk at women with short hair everywhere, trying to decide what style would look best on me. Finally, last May, I decided to do it.

I chose the last day of my exams, which was the next month, because I didn't want too many friends seeing me with short hair before I had a chance to see it. Hee Won agreed to go with me because I would have probably chickened out if she didn't. We walked around my neighborhood, trying to find a good but cheap salon. I almost hoped we wouldn't succeed. My stomach was queasy. (Do 16-year-olds get ulcers?) But we did. The sign said, "$10 for cut, any length."

Cutting my hair was my way of rebelling against my parents. Now I had to go home and face them.

When we went inside, Hee Won and I looked through a magazine for a style. I found a model with a really cropped cut and pointed her out to the hair-cutter. Then I sat down in a chair and the stylist put a white sheet around me. I took a deep breath, trying to relax. He released my hair from the ponytail I had stuffed it into. He sprayed water on it. I babbled nervously to Hee Won. Then he started cutting.

The worst part was the crunchy sound when he first chopped off about six inches of my hair. I thought that maybe I should tell him not to go any further. I could see my hair all around me on the floor. (And at any moment, my lunch might have joined it.) I guess my nervousness showed because the haircutter smiled and said, "You won't be needing that anymore." Easy for him to say. He and Hee Won were casually singing along to the radio, while I was scared to death.

For the next part, he told me to take my glasses off. I'm half-blind so I couldn't even see my reflection clearly in the mirror, let alone what he was doing. But I took my glasses off anyway. By now, I had decided I should go all the way. Besides, how short could it be?

The next time I put my glasses back on, it was already over. Too late to change my mind. "Oh, sh-t," I thought, looking into the mirror.

I didn't know it would be this short. It was so short that some of my hair was sticking up. The stylist told me that was because my hair had to get used to being that short. Forget the hair, what about my parents? Panic time. Hee Won told me it looked great. I nodded distractedly and paid up my $10. The whole affair had taken about 20 minutes.

I walked outside and immediately felt that everyone was staring at me. "It's because you look great," I told myself. Yeah, right. It looked horrible, I wasn't meant to have short hair, it would never grow back, my parents would kill me....

Cutting my hair was my way of rebelling against my parents. What I didn't realize was that it was only half the struggle. Now I had to go home and face them.

My dad was on the phone as I came into the living room. "What happened?" he said.

"I got a haircut," I said lightly, trying not to sound nervous. He was silent so I went to my room. I listened to the radio and paced. I stared at myself in the mirror, trying to get used to the new me.

When my mom walked in, I was reading a book. She stared for a moment. "I don't like it one bit," she said. "It screws up your whole face." I didn't know what to say, so I pretended to ignore her. I wasn't hoping for an "It looks great...I'm glad you did it," but I wasn't expecting anything that cruel. Later I told my friends that since she didn't like it, I probably looked great. I was lying, of course.

I consoled myself, thinking that at least my dad didn't say anything. Then I overheard him talking about my "awful haircut." Later that night, my mom told me that he yelled at her for "letting" me cut my hair.

My friends' reactions were more diverse, ranging from "I couldn't recognize you from the back!" to "You should be in Vogue modeling that haircut." A close friend, who is Indian and had hair almost down to her waist, wasn't too thrilled, but she said she was "getting used to it."

I tried to tell myself that it didn't matter what my relatives thought. But I was really hurt by their insensitive comments.

Another friend said, "You look butch." Huh? "You know," she explained, "in a lesbian relationship, it's the partner who plays the male role." Oh? I didn't know cutting your hair meant changing your sexual preference.

Five days after my haircut, I went to New Orleans to visit my relatives. Given my parents' reaction, I was very nervous about what they would say. My aunt freaked. "I can't believe you cut your hair," she said, turning to my uncle. "She had such pretty hair." I still did. "I can't believe you cut your hair. You had such pretty hair..." Okay, I got your point already.

This was how my uncle introduced me to a guest at his house: "This is my nephew...uh...I mean niece," he said. Ha, ha.

It got better. "She had long hair before," he explained. "I guess she hates to be beautiful." What the hell was that supposed to mean? That I was ugly now? I became convinced that the haircut was a huge mistake. I tried to tell myself that it didn't matter what my relatives thought. But I was really hurt by their insensitive comments.

We drove up to Atlanta to visit more family. The first thing Uncle 2 said was, "You've changed." Fair enough. Then Uncle 1 (of New Orleans) said, "She fell asleep at the hair salon and this is what happened." That's not what happened, I protested, but they were too busy laughing.

Back in New York, I told anyone who would listen what my relatives had said. My friends consoled me by saying that they were just jerks. It took me about two weeks to get used to the cut and a month to realize short hair was right for me. As a kid, I had short hair because it was my mom's idea, and I let it grow out because she wanted me to. This time, I'll keep it short because I like the way I look.

Needing my mom's help to style my hair made me feel young and vulnerable. But now, I can style it myself (if you can call running a comb through it a couple of times "styling"). It is fun to run my hands through my hair and not worry about getting it tangled. It feels great to wash and dry my hair in less than 15 minutes. I'm the kind of person who feels more comfortable in jeans and t-shirts than in dresses, so my new no-fuss hairstyle fits my lifestyle.

Since I've gotten my hair cut, I've learnt a few things about beauty, too. I know that being "beautiful" has nothing to do with the length of my hair and that a short cut has nothing to do with being gay or straight. Friends tell me I look older with short hair. Better yet, I feel older and more secure about myself. In spite of my parents' reservations and my relatives' stereotypes, I'm glad I cut my hair.

Anita was 16 when she wrote this story. After high school she went to Swarthmore College and earned a PhD in Education from the University of Pennsylvania.

Cezary Ladocha

Moonlit Memories

By Chun Lar Tom

One evening, back in China, my little sister Bik Bik and I sat in front of our house to wait for the moon. An hour later, the moon rose. The village became beautiful and charming in the softness of the moonlight.

"Let's go tell Mom to get ready for the Moon Festival celebration!" Bik Bik yelled and ran into the house.

Moon Festival is also called Mid-Autumn Day (Zhong Qiu Jie). It's usually held at night during a full moon on the fifteenth day of the eighth lunar month. That night, the moon is believed to be at its brightest and roundest for the year. In China, people consider this the best time to celebrate the end of the harvest season with a big feast.

That evening, Bik Bik and I helped Mom set up a table in the open air near our house, like the rest of the people in our village.

We ate dishes like chicken and river snails with red pepper. After dinner, Father set off firecrackers and burned incense to welcome the goddess of the moon, the Moon Lady.

For dessert, we ate mooncakes, the most important food served because they symbolize the festival. Like their name implies, mooncakes are usually round like the moon. To me, mooncakes also symbolized family unity and perfection. Every year at the Moon Festival, my aunts, uncles, and cousins who worked and lived miles away in the city of KaiPing would come to my village of Maoping with delicious mooncakes.

I could never forget the whole family sitting at the table, eating mooncakes, chatting and laughing in the soft moonlight. It was a feeling of reunion, harmonious and joyful. Aunt Mei laughed loudest at the table. She was a kind and happy person with a big smile on her face all the time. And cute, fat Uncle Qiang was my favorite little uncle. His big eyes shone on his round face as he told us about the circus he saw in the city. Then there was my cousin Yi, a sweet and quiet girl who followed me everywhere during the festival. When she smiled, two dimples lit up her ruddy oval face.

Our grandparents had told us that the Moon Lady was supposed to come down to Earth and eat the mooncakes that people prepared for her.

"Mom, how do you know the Moon Lady came down and ate the mooncakes already?" Bik Bik asked as we ate dessert.

"I just know it," Mom replied. Mom told us stories about the Moon Lady and taught us folk songs to invite her. And Grandma showed us how to make wishes to the Moon Lady. Bik Bik and I were always running around during the festival, humming songs, eating our mooncakes.

My memories of the Moon Festival are some of the warmest memories I have of my family. But things changed after I came to America when I was 15. My family members and I are no longer able to get together. My aged grandparents, Aunt Mei, and Uncle Qiang are all back in China.

When the night of the Moon Festival came during my first year in America, I missed them all so much, especially my grandparents. My family here can't celebrate the Moon Festival the way we used to. We can't set up a table in the open air like we did in Maoping, watching the moon as we enjoyed our mooncakes. And now, for dinner on the day of the festival, Mom cooks shrimp instead of river snails, because that's what's available.

The mooncakes' roundness reminds me that my family isn't round and whole anymore.

We still eat mooncakes on the night of the festival. But for me, after losing my traditions, mooncakes can't symbolize family unity any more. When I look at the designs on its skin, which looked beautiful back in Maoping, they seem like little cracks that'll split the cake apart. The mooncakes' roundness reminds me that my family isn't round and whole anymore.

During the last mooncake celebration I had with my family in Brooklyn, I looked up into the dark blue sky, mooncake in hand. The moon didn't look as bright and round as it did in China. Taking a small bite of the mooncake, I heard my grandmom's soft voice coming from overseas.

"Chun Lar, make your wish to the Moon Lady. It will come true."

I stared at the moon and made my wish: "I wish my family will be reunited for the next Moon Festival."

Chun Lar was 18 when she wrote this story.
She later attended Bard College.

YC Art Dept.

Piecing Together Our History

By Priscilla Chan

The Yung Wing Public School—that was my elementary school. For seven years, I went there every day; walked up the front steps and saw that name printed on the front of the building. And never during those seven years did I know who Yung Wing was.

Five years later, I finally found out the identity of my school's namesake. Yung Wing became the first Chinese graduate of an American university when he received his B.A. from Yale University in 1855. So I guess it was fitting to name a school after him. I got the answer to that question and learned much more about the history of the Chinese people in North, Central, and South America during a visit to the Museum of Chinese in America, in New York City.

For me, a trip to the museum was a fascinating look at history through the eyes of the Chinese. It had never really dawned on me how much of an impact the Chinese have made in the Americas. Not only that, but it also showed me how to trace my roots to my first ancestor on these lands. For someone who never looked farther back than her grandparents when constructing a family tree, that was a big achievement.

The museum first tries to help people understand why the Chinese migrated here. The "push factors" were a deteriorating economy, floods, famine, and government corruption in 19th century China. To find a better place to settle, thousands of Chinese endured the strenuous voyage to the New World.

When they arrived, the reception they received here was hardly warm or open. The first immigrants worked night and day to make ends meet. In Peru, they shoveled bird droppings that were used as fertilizer; in Trinidad, they harvested sugar cane; in the United States, they built railroads, washed and ironed clothing, and served food.

They realized almost instantly that their living conditions would not be much different here than in China. Instead of a better life, they encountered brutal working conditions, racial discrimination, and limited economic mobility.

The U.S. government passed several statutes permitting discrimination against the Chinese.

The museum depicts the vivid history of Chinese people in the Americas with a timeline that runs through the exhibit. It starts in the year 1785 when three Chinese seamen landed in Baltimore (the first recorded instance of Chinese people arriving in the United States) and ends in 1993 with the grounding of the immigrant-carrying vessel Golden Venture off Far Rockaway, New York.

It's what's between these two dates that's most important, though. Did you know who helped the most in building the Transcontinental Railroad? Chinese workers (between 1863 and 1869). Did you know where the Bing cherry got its name? From a Chinese farmer named Ah Bing who first grew this special cherry in 1875.

Did you know that the U.S. government passed several statutes in less than a century permitting discrimination against the Chinese? They included the Scott Act, passed in 1888, which prohibited the re-entry of 20,000 Chinese workers who temporarily left the country even though they had received permits to return before leaving.

Also, did you know the first U.S. restriction on immigration based solely on race and nationality was against the Chinese people? The Chinese Exclusion Act of 1882 restricted Chinese immigration to the U.S. and denied the Chinese the right to become American citizens.

The museum holds the story of a people told in pictures and words. One of the most amazing objects in the exhibit is a collage, carefully cut and pieced together from several different photographs and perfectly pasted together so that the final piece appears to be a family portrait. There are about 15 people, from three generations, all seemingly posed on a happy family occasion.

However, the true story was that the family had been separated; some had come to the Americas and some had stayed behind. It was only by cutting their faces out from different pictures that they could be joined together in one family portrait.

Looking at where the people are standing and how they appear in relation to each other, you can see the delicate hand of the anonymous person who painstakingly pieced this image together. You can also see how important family is in Chinese culture, that someone could create such a masterpiece in hopes that one day, his or her family would really be together.

Another object on display that struck me as very central to Chinese history was a slipper for a bound foot. Binding the feet of females to restrict their growth, beginning at birth, was a long-accepted custom in Chinese culture. It was believed the smaller her foot, the more beautiful a woman was. It was not unusual to have girls screaming in pain from their disgustingly misshapen feet.

I swear the slipper in the exhibit is at most three inches long, the length of my index finger. Walking by the display, I could hear the other museum-goers gasp at the shoe, understandably, of course. It is a painful reminder of how far the Chinese have come in adopting modern standards. To give you an idea of how recently this custom was abolished, my great-grandmother had her feet bound. It was only my grandmother's generation that started believing that it was no longer necessary to do it.

The museum also devotes many sections of the exhibit to Chinese successes in the Americas. The timeline includes the year Amy Tan's novel *The Joy Luck Club* became a major motion picture; the year Michael Chang, then 17, became the youngest tennis player to win the French Open; and the year Maya Lin designed the Vietnam Memorial.

There is also a youth section which includes items a student advisory council selected to represent the interests of Chinese-American youth. These include music, books, sports equipment, a pair of nunchucks, and a bookbag.

If you're in New York City, I would highly recommend taking the trip to Chinatown, spending a few hours taking in the exhibits, and capping off the day with dinner at a Chinese restaurant. What could be better than seeing history through cool objects, beautiful art, and poignant photographs, and at the same time, learning something about the people who will make your delicious dinner that evening? I guarantee it'll be a day full of fascination and satisfaction.

To learn more about the Museum of Chinese in America, go to www.mocanyc.org.

Priscilla wrote this story when she was 17. She later earned a degree in environmental science and public policy from Harvard University, and became a high school science teacher.

Teens:
How to Get More Out of This Book

Self-help: The teens who wrote the stories in this book did so because they hope that telling their stories will help readers who are facing similar challenges. They want you to know that you are not alone, and that taking specific steps can help you manage or overcome very difficult situations. They've done their best to be clear about the actions that worked for them so you can see if they'll work for you.

Writing: You can also use the book to improve your writing skills. Each teen in this book wrote 5-10 drafts of his or her story before it was published. If you read the stories closely you'll see that the teens work to include a beginning, a middle, and an end, and good scenes, description, dialogue, and anecdotes (little stories). To improve your writing, take a look at how these writers construct their stories. Try some of their techniques in your own writing.

Resources on the Web

We will occasionally post Think About It questions on our website, www.youthcomm.org, to accompany stories in this and other Youth Communication books. We try out the questions with teens and post the ones they like best. Many teens report that writing answers to those questions in a journal is very helpful.

How to Use This Book in Staff Training

Staff say that reading these stories gives them greater insight into what teens are thinking and feeling, and new strategies for working with them. You can help the staff you work with by using these stories as case studies.

Select one story to read in the group, and ask staff to identify and discuss the main issue facing the teen. There may be disagreement about this, based on the background and experience of staff. That is fine. One point of the exercise is that teens have complex lives and needs. Adults can probably be more effective if they don't focus too narrowly and can see several dimensions of their clients.

Ask staff: What issues or feelings does the story provoke in them? What kind of help do they think the teen wants? What interventions are likely to be most promising? Least effective? Why? How would you build trust with the teen writer? How have other adults failed the teen, and how might that affect his or her willingness to accept help? What other resources would be helpful to this teen, such as peer support, a mentor, counseling, family therapy, etc?

Resources on the Web

From time to time we will post Think About It questions on our website, www.youthcomm.org, to accompany stories in this and other Youth Communication books. We try out the questions with teens and post the ones that they find most effective. We'll also post lessons for some of the stories. Adults can use the questions and lessons in workshops.

Discussion Guide

Teachers and Staff:
How to Use This Book in Groups

When working with teens individually or in groups, you can use these stories to help young people face difficult issues in a way that feels safe to them. That's because talking about the issues in the stories usually feels safer to teens than talking about those same issues in their own lives. Addressing issues through the stories allows for some personal distance; they hit close to home, but not too close. Talking about them opens up a safe place for reflection. As teens gain confidence talking about the issues in the stories, they usually become more comfortable talking about those issues in their own lives.

Below are general questions to guide your discussion. In most cases you can read a story and conduct a discussion in one 45-minute session. Teens are usually happy to read the stories aloud, with each teen reading a paragraph or two. (Allow teens to pass if they don't want to read.) It takes 10-15 minutes to read a story straight through. However, it is often more effective to let workshop participants make comments and discuss the story as you go along. The workshop leader may even want to annotate her copy of the story beforehand with key questions.

If teens read the story ahead of time or silently, it's good to break the ice with a few questions that get everyone on the same page: Who is the main character? How old is she? What happened to her? How did she respond? Another good starting question is: "What stood out for you in the story?" Go around the room and let each person briefly mention one thing.

Then move on to open-ended questions, which encourage participants to think more deeply about what the writers were feeling, the choices they faced, and the actions they took. There are no right or wrong answers to the open-ended questions.

Open-ended questions encourage participants to think about how the themes, emotions, and choices in the stories relate to their own lives. Here are some examples of open-ended questions that we have found to be effective. You can use variations of these questions with almost any story in this book.

—What main problem or challenge did the writer face?

—What choices did the teen have in trying to deal with the problem?

—Which way of dealing with the problem was most effective for the teen? Why?

—What strengths, skills, or resources did the teen use to address the challenge?

—If you were in the writer's shoes, what would you have done?

—What could adults have done better to help this young person?

—What have you learned by reading this story that you didn't know before?

—What, if anything, will you do differently after reading this story?

—What surprised you in this story?

—Do you have a different view of this issue, or see a different way of dealing with it, after reading this story? Why or why not?

Credits

The stories in this book originally appeared in the following Youth Communication publications:

"Fighting the 'Model Minority' Stereotype," by Jordan Yue, *New Youth Connections*, January/February 2004; "Chinese Parents, American Me," by Ngan-Fong Huang, *New Youth Connections*, April 1997; "Tongue-Tied," by Amy Huang, *New Youth Connections*, September/October 2002; "My Life as an ABC," by Victoria Law, *New Youth Connections*, May/June 1995; "Ignoring the Stares," by Leneli Liggayu, *New Youth Connections*, November 2007; "Where Nobody Knows My Name," by Sung Park, *New Youth Connections*, May/June 1995; "Beyond the Great Wall of Chinatown," by Xiao Ling Zhong, *New Youth Connections*, November 1998; "'Chinklish,'" by Winnie Tang, *New Youth Connections*, September/October 2001; "Wake-Up Call in Another World," by Maria Zaman, *New Youth Connections*, December 2004; "Unwelcome in the Hood," by George Yi, *New Youth Connections*, December 1995; "What's a Girl Worth?" by May Mai, *New Youth Connections*, September/October 2005; "Dreams of America, Memories of China," by Chun Lar Tom, *New Youth Connections*, April 2002; "Thinking Twice About Race," by Luce Tang, *New Youth Connections*, April 2004; "Holding on to Who I Am," by Zaineb Nadeem, *New Youth Connections*, May/June 2004; "My Korean Boyfriend," by Sue Chong, *New Youth Connections*, November 1991; "The Stranger in My House," by May Mai, *New Youth Connections*, May/June 2005; "Chinese in America, American in China," by Kim Hoang, *New Youth Connections*, May/June 1995; "Other Ways to be Rich," by Leneli Liggayu, *New Youth Connections*, September/October 2006; "Money Can't Buy Love," by Lily Mai, *New Youth Connections*, December 2005; "A Short Cut to Independence," by Anita Chikkaur, *New Youth Connections*, September/October 1994; "Moon Festival Memories," by Chun Lar Tom, *New Youth Connections*, November 2002; "Piecing Together Our History," by Priscilla Chan, *New Youth Connections*, November 1996.

About Youth Communication

Youth Communication, founded in 1980, is a nonprofit youth development program located in New York City whose mission is to teach writing, journalism, and leadership skills. The teenagers we train become writers for our websites and books and for two print magazines: *New Youth Connections,* a general-interest youth magazine, and *Represent,* a magazine by and for young people in foster care.

Each year, up to 100 young people participate in Youth Communication's school-year and summer journalism workshops, where they work under the direction of full-time professional editors. Most are African-American, Latino, or Asian, and many are recent immigrants. The opportunity to reach their peers with accurate portrayals of their lives and important self-help information motivates the young writers to create powerful stories.

Our goal is to run a strong youth development program in which teens produce high quality stories that inform and inspire their peers. Doing so requires us to be sensitive to the complicated lives and emotions of the teen participants while also providing an intellectually rigorous experience. We achieve that goal in the writing/teaching/editing relationship, which is the core of our program.

Our teaching and editorial process begins with discussions

between adult editors and the teen staff. In those meetings, the teens and the editors work together to identify the most important issues in the teens' lives and to figure out how those issues can be turned into stories that will resonate with teen readers.

Once story topics are chosen, students begin the process of crafting their stories. For a personal story, that means revisiting events in one's past to understand their significance for the future. For a commentary, it means developing a logical and persuasive point of view. For a reported story, it means gathering information through research and interviews. Students look inward and outward as they try to make sense of their experiences and the world around them and find the points of intersection between personal and social concerns. That process can take a few weeks or a few months. Stories frequently go through 10 or more drafts as students work under the guidance of their editors, the way any professional writer does.

Many of the students who walk through our doors have uneven skills, as a result of poor education, living under extremely stressful conditions, or coming from homes where English is a second language. Yet, to complete their stories, students must successfully perform a wide range of activities, including writing and rewriting, reading, discussion, reflection, research, interviewing, and typing. They must work as members of a team and they must accept individual responsibility. They learn to provide constructive criticism, and to accept it. They engage in explorations of truthfulness, fairness, and accuracy. They meet deadlines. They must develop the audacity to believe that they have something important to say and the humility to recognize that saying it well is not a process of instant gratification. Rather, it usually requires a long, hard struggle through many discussions and much rewriting.

It would be impossible to teach these skills and dispositions as separate, disconnected topics, like grammar, ethics, or assertiveness. However, we find that students make rapid progress when they are learning skills in the context of an inquiry that is personally significant to them and that will benefit their peers.

When teens publish their stories—in *New Youth Connections* and *Represent,* on the Web, and in other publications—they reach tens of thousands of teen and adult readers. Teachers, counselors, social workers, and other adults circulate the stories to young people in their classes and out-of-school youth programs. Adults tell us that teens in their programs—including many who are ordinarily resistant to reading—clamor for the stories. Teen readers report that the stories give them information they can't get anywhere else, and inspire them to reflect on their lives and open lines of communication with adults.

Writers usually participate in our program for one semester, though some stay much longer. Years later, many of them report that working here was a turning point in their lives—that it helped them acquire the confidence and skills that they needed for success in college and careers. Scores of our graduates have overcome tremendous obstacles to become journalists, writers, and novelists. They include National Book Award finalist and MacArthur Fellowship winner Edwidge Danticat, novelist Ernesto Quiñonez, writer Veronica Chambers, and *New York Times* reporter Rachel Swarns. Hundreds more are working in law, business, and other careers. Many are teachers, principals, and youth workers, and several have started nonprofit youth programs themselves and work as mentors—helping another generation of young people develop their skills and find their voices.

Youth Communication is a nonprofit educational corporation. Contributions are gratefully accepted and are tax deductible to the fullest extent of the law.

To make a contribution, or for information about our publications and programs, including our catalog of over 100 books and curricula for hard-to-reach teens, see www.youthcomm.org.

About the Editors

Maria Luisa Tucker is the associate editor of *New Youth Connections,* Youth Communication's magazine by and for New York City teens. Before coming to Youth Communication, she worked as a reporter for the *Village Voice*. She has also written for several other publications, including *AlterNet.org,* an online magazine, and the *Santa Fe Reporter,* a weekly newspaper where her work garnered several awards for investigative and media reporting. She holds a bachelor's degree in journalism from Texas State University and a master's in American Studies from Columbia University.

Keith Hefner co-founded Youth Communication in 1980 and has directed it ever since. He is the recipient of the Luther P. Jackson Education Award from the New York Association of Black Journalists and a MacArthur Fellowship. He was also a Revson Fellow at Columbia University.

Laura Longhine is the editorial director at Youth Communication. She edited *Represent,* Youth Communication's magazine by and for youth in foster care, for three years, and has written for a variety of publications. She has a BA in English from Tufts University and an MS in Journalism from Columbia University.

More Helpful Books From Youth Communication

The Struggle to Be Strong: True Stories by Teens About Overcoming Tough Times. Foreword by Veronica Chambers. Help young people identify and build on their own strengths with 30 personal stories about resiliency. (Free Spirit)

Starting With "I": Personal Stories by Teenagers. "Who am I and who do I want to become?" Thirty-five stories examine this question through the lens of race, ethnicity, gender, sexuality, family, and more. Increase this book's value with the free Teacher's Guide, available from youthcomm.org. (Youth Communication)

Real Stories, Real Teens. Inspire teens to read and recognize their strengths with this collection of 26 true stories by teens. The young writers describe how they overcame significant challenges and stayed true to themselves. Also includes the first chapters from three novels in the Bluford Series. (Youth Communication)

The Courage to Be Yourself: True Stories by Teens About Cliques, Conflicts, and Overcoming Peer Pressure. In 26 first-person stories, teens write about their lives with searing honesty. These stories will inspire young readers to reflect on their own lives, work through their problems, and help them discover who they really are. (Free Spirit)

Out With It: Gay and Straight Teens Write About Homosexuality. Break stereotypes and provide support with this unflinching look at gay life from a teen's perspective. With a focus on urban youth, this book also includes several heterosexual teens' transformative experiences with gay peers. (Youth Communication)

Things Get Hectic: Teens Write About the Violence That Surrounds Them. Violence is commonplace in many teens' lives, be it bullying, gangs, dating, or family relationships. Hear the experiences of victims, perpetrators, and witnesses through more than 50 real-world stories. (Youth Communication)

From Dropout to Achiever: Teens Write About School. Help teens overcome the challenges of graduating, which may involve overcoming family problems, bouncing back from a bad semester, or even dropping out for a time. These teens show how they achieve academic success. (Youth Communication)

Growing Up Black: Teens Write About African-American Identity. Your teens will want to share their own experiences when they read these true stories about family, friendship, sexuality, popular culture, city life, hair, and yes, racism.

Growing Up Latino: Teens Write About Hispanic-American Identity. What does it mean to be a Latino teen? Spur a discussion with these stories about real experiences with family, ethnic pride, and cultural conflict.

Growing Up Muslim in America: Stories by Muslim Youth. Teens of all backgrounds will appreciate these true stories that tackle the issues of invisibility, discrimination, arranged marriage, and pride in the Muslim faith.

Through Thick and Thin: Teens Write About Obesity, Eating Disorders, and Self Image. Help teens who struggle with obesity, eating disorders, and body weight issues. These stories show the pressures teens face when they are confronted by unrealistic standards for physical appearance, and how emotions can affect the way we eat. (Youth Communication)

To order these and other books, go to:
www.youthcomm.org
or call 212-279-0708 x115

www.ingramcontent.com/pod-product-compliance
Lightning Source LLC
Chambersburg PA
CBHW052215270326
41931CB00011B/2358

9781935552352